25 ROLE PLAYS FOR ASSERTIVENESS TRAINING

25 ROLE PLAYS FOR ASSERTIVENESS TRAINING

Sue Bishop

Gower

First published 1993 by Gower Publishing

This paperback edition published 1995 by
Gower Publishing
Gower House
Croft Road
Aldershot
Hants GU11 3HR
England

Gower
Old Post Road
Brookfield
Vermont 05036
USA

CIP catalogue records for this book are available from the British Library

ISBN 0-566-07681-0

Typeset in 12pt Century Old Style by Poole Typesetting (Wessex) Ltd, Bournemouth, Dorset.
Printed in Great Britain by Antony Rowe Ltd, Chippenham, Wiltshire.

Contents

Preface

When compiling this manual of role plays I made the assumption that the trainer would be either running a course on assertiveness, or using assertion as a session on a course with a wider brief. I have also assumed that such a trainer would be experienced in the subject, and would not, therefore, need instruction on basics such as:

- terminology
- definitions
- listening skills
- non-verbal communication and body language

... and so on.

However, a summary of the key techniques may be useful and can be found on page ix.

Here I should make clear my own views on assertiveness training. I firmly believe that it is of immense benefit to a large number of people, not just as a skill in itself, but as a means to improved confidence, enhanced self-esteem and honest, powerful and effective communication.

In most publications on assertiveness training a 'Bill of Rights' (see page xiii) appears in varying forms. Most include statements such as: 'I have the right to ask for what I want.' I feel that the antithesis to this is equally true, and these opposites should also be included in the 'Rights': i.e. '*You* also have the right to ask for what you want'. It should be understood that acknowledgement of the other person's viewpoint is vitally important to successful assertive behaviour. Similarly, although *you* have the right to ask for what you want, *I* have an equal right to refuse you that request.

For me, assertion means having the confidence to communicate without becoming aggressive, or producing aggression in others. It means respecting others' views without losing one's own self-respect, or losing sight of one's own needs. It means standing firm on issues which are important, but being prepared to co-operate, compromise and negotiate to reach a 'win/win' conclusion on other less important matters. It means working towards balanced discussions, making one's own view clear, while allowing the other person to do the same.

Assertiveness training is part of self-development. The role plays practised in the supportive environment of the training room represent the tip of an exciting iceberg – a lifelong adventure in increased self-awareness, better understanding of what makes others 'tick', and how best to communicate and interact. Trainees should be made aware of the need to constantly practise, evaluate exchanges, re-evaluate possible approaches and so on. This is so much easier if there is on-going support and advice from someone close. It should be recognised that assertiveness training, if effective, will necessarily have an impact on existing relationships, and virtually every human interaction. It follows that results of training should be implemented gradually, and with sensitivity with all whom it may affect – partners, friends, relatives and so on.

I hope that this collection of role plays will be useful to trainers, and provide participants with a challenging and enjoyable introduction to assertiveness training.

Sue Bishop

Summary of key techniques

The following is a brief summary of the main techniques used in assertiveness training. They are organized under headings that correspond to the way the role plays in this manual are grouped.

Broken record

A technique used where participants need to be persistent in their assertions. Without necessarily using the same words over and over parrot-fashion, participants can practise building their confidence by staying calm and keeping to the point they wish to make, reiterating this point for as long as it takes. They should avoid becoming diverted by persuasive argument or entering into lengthy discussion, explanation or excuses.

Saying 'No'

Interpersonal relationships can suffer unless refusing a request is delivered properly and with respect for the self-esteem of both parties. Participants practise this technique so that *if* they decide to refuse a request, they can say 'No' with confidence, and without ambiguity or hostility.

Setting limits

Similar to 'saying "No"' and 'broken record', this technique will probably involve an element of both. Setting limits helps participants to take ownership of their own needs, accept their own capabilities, and articulate their unique boundaries: 'I will go so far, and no further.' Setting limits is letting the other person know what you are prepared to do (or not do) and how you expect to be treated.

Asking for what we want

This is everyone's right, and *how* you ask often determines success or failure. By practising this technique, participants will realize that asking does not always mean getting, but by expressing rather than repressing a need, self-esteem is sustained.

Dealing with the talkative person

A technique to use so that the person concerned will not feel hurt or rejected; conversely, you don't spend ages listening to an endless outpouring of irrelevances. Participants practise the art of keeping the talkative person on target.

Dealing with the angry person

The role plays in this manual are designed for working situations, hence, dealing with an angry or aggressive person, whether a colleague, client or boss, is more than likely to arise. Participants using this technique will learn to recognize the cause of the outburst, how to reduce tension arising from it, and how to pacify the person concerned. This is not to say that personal, abusive onslaughts have to be tolerated, but considerations such as the need to keep one's job have to be taken into account.

Handling your own anger

By saying 'I am really angry about …' rather than showing that anger by tantrums, or sulking, or sarcasm, begins the process of communication rather than confrontation – a technique which should be practised. The technique is equally important for people who find it difficult to express anger in any form, but repress it, causing stress and tension within themselves.

Dealing with sexual harassment

One person's teasing is another's harassment; what one person can accept in the behaviour of others, another can find threatening. Sexual harassment is therefore difficult to define, but where it is encountered techniques can be practised to deal assertively with the unwanted attention or offensive comments.

Dealing with money matters

Negotiating a starting salary at recruitment interview, pricing your services, asking for financial help from government departments and so on prove difficult and embarrassing for most people, so participants can practise using their assertiveness skills to recognize and articulate self-value and their right to fair treatment.

Self-assertion

This technique develops self-marketing, specifically in the interview situation. Participants should recognize and be able to 'sell' their qualities, achievements, skills and attributes in an appropriate assertive way.

Everyone's Bill of Rights

To be treated with respect as a capable and equal human being

To have and express your own feelings, values and opinions without having to justify, or make apologies

To be listened to and taken seriously

To set your own priorities and state your own needs and to be yourself; not necessarily what other people expect or want you to be

To say 'yes' or 'no' for yourself without feeling guilty or selfish

To have the right to make mistakes and to change your mind sometimes

To ask for what you want while accepting that asking does not always mean getting

To say 'I don't understand'

To choose not to assert yourself

Introduction

It is generally agreed amongst trainers that role plays are the simplest and most effective way for participants to reinforce learning and practise assertiveness techniques. Role plays are one way to fulfil the 'doing' element of the Tell, Show, Do method of training, usually associated with skills training, but also applicable to the assertiveness model. They are particularly useful in assertiveness training in that they allow participants to try various approaches, to experiment with the feel of different phraseology, volume or tone of voice, to test out the reaction of others, and to get constructive feedback on their communication skills – all in the safe environment of the training room.

When using role plays, it is essential that sufficient trainer input is first given on the theories of the assertiveness model, and on the techniques to be practised. This, of course, is the 'tell' element of the Tell, Show, Do approach. The introductions to the techniques covered in this book, to be found at the start of each section, are not intended to replace this important element on assertiveness training programmes.

All the role plays in this manual are intended as introductions to various assertiveness techniques. The scenarios – all business centred – have, of necessity, to be on general themes. Once participants are comfortable with each technique, it is important that further practise, on issues relevant to them, be offered as a follow up to the off-the-peg exercises provided here.

Whatever the context, and whoever constructs them, all role plays are artificial to some extent; acting is involved by one or both of the players. If a participant has difficulty with, or feels he/she has failed in a role play, it is easy to put the blame on this artificiality. 'I can't be natural, acting this out in front of others' or 'I wouldn't have done it that way back at work' or 'I wouldn't say that if this were real life' are the sorts of remarks which spring from defensiveness. Comments such as these may arise when using off-the-peg role plays. However, criticism can be reduced by explaining that they

- are carefully constructed to bring out the learning points
- are as near to real life as possible given the constraints which exist
- are a means of practising techniques in a supportive environment with the benefit of peer and trainer feedback
- will be followed by role rehearsals of issues directly relevant to course participants.

My intention has been to give trainers as much help and guidance as possible in both the running and processing of these role plays. To this end I have provided:

Introductions. Each section has a brief explanation of the technique to be practised. Trainers may wish to photocopy and distribute this as an additional handout.

Briefing sheets. These are provided for all 'actors'. They set the scene, indicate what is required of the 'actor', and suggest how to start or maintain the role play should participants be short of ideas of their own.

Observer brief. These give the scenario and some indication of what to expect from the interaction. Various questions are posed which can, if desired, be used by the trainer to guide processing. This, of course, is optional. Some trainers may want more spontaneity than the briefs allow.

Trainer's notes. These give processing guidance, and suggest a line of questioning which develops the participants' understanding of the role play. These are, of necessity, general, because it is impossible to foresee how each role play will proceed. This will depend on the 'actors' and the information and experience each individual brings to the situation. The notes do not presume to be inclusive, and are intended as a guide only.

Example dialogues. These, too, can be photocopied and distributed to participants, and could form part of the 'show' element of the Tell, Show, Do approach if desired.

Handouts. In addition to the above information which can be duplicated and distributed, there are general handouts with 'Do's' and 'Don'ts' tips covering most of the techniques described.

OBJECTIVES

After acting in, or observing, each role play, participants should:

- understand that assertiveness involves at least two people; and that for every right *one* person has, the other person has exactly similar rights
- be aware that assertiveness is not competitive, nor is it employed to achieve one's own way, to win or to lose, or to establish one-upmanship. The objective is better understanding and clearer, more honest communication
- realize that assertiveness increases confidence and self-esteem which in turn improves the quality of communication with others
- be able to recognize, and therefore anticipate, obstacles to assertive behaviour
- realize that assertiveness means taking responsibility for their own lives, feelings and actions
- be able to better direct a discussion on an adult/adult basis, making their own point while allowing others to do the same.

APPLICATIONS

The role plays described are about good, sound communication practices from which anyone can benefit – men and women, staff and management. They can be applied to help you identify what you want, and how to express this need, calmly and clearly rather than relying on hints, or the other person guessing what you feel, or expecting him or her to know what you want by intuition!

The role plays are all set in the business world, so they will be appropriate for management courses. However, the principles tested by the exercises are common to basic assertiveness training – the skills practised and learned apply to any situation demanding sensible and sensitive communication, in or out of the workplace.

CONTENT

With any effective communication, it is difficult to isolate and examine tightly-defined areas. For example, 'Saying "No"' will almost certainly involve practising the 'broken record' technique, and reflecting back. It can involve setting limits, can involve asking for what you want, can involve cooperation, could involve compromise or negotiation. There will, therefore, be overlaps in the role plays. However, an attempt has been made to group the scenarios which have similar themes, such as dealing with difficult or problem people, like the over-talkative individual, or the angry person. The manual has role plays on handling your own anger, dealing with sexual harassment, and on money matters, as well as more general themes like asking for what you want, saying 'No', and setting limits.

There are aspects of assertiveness that this manual does not cover. I have chosen to concentrate on the subjects selected so that several examples of each can be given. In this way, if there is an opportunity for more than one pair to practise, say, 'broken record' on your course, another role play is readily available. It may be more appropriate for participants to work in small groups on your course. Again, several different role plays on the same theme are available.

A point about the section 'Dealing with Money Matters'. Of necessity, sums of money, rates per hour or day, and so on have been supplied to give realism to the role plays. This has the disadvantage of fixing the role plays in place and time. The currency quoted is sterling, and the rates are appropriate to the date of publication. Trainers should amend these role plays as required before using them with their groups.

RUNNING THE ROLE PLAYS

How much, or how little, is given to the principal players by way of briefing sheets, prior instruction, and so on is, of course, in the hands of the trainer. For example, you may decide to provide props – such as chairs (or choice of chairs!) – where appropriate, or a telephone where the role play calls for it. Obviously, the most important factors are to create a supportive environment and to explain fully the importance of role play to the learning process.

If these role plays are used as part of a course where participants already have a fair knowledge of aspects of assertion such as intonation, volume, choice of words, body language, non-verbal messages and so on, it may be useful to give a different task to one or more group members (as well as general observations). For example: 'Jon and Anne, watch out for choice of words, noting down where you felt a different option might have produced a different reaction. Rakesh and Helen, could you keep a note of body language ...'.

It may be helpful for participants acting out the scenarios to use their own names. Of necessity, I have had to give names to the characters, which ideally would not have been gender-specific. However, finding over 50 unisex names proved impossible – even unisex names become gender-specific when written down, e.g. Frances/Francis or Bobbie/Bobby. In addition, the usage of her/his and she/him throughout would have looked clumsy and hindered understanding. With the possible exception of the role plays on sexual harassment, participants should be able to undertake all roles, irrespective of the gender suggested by the names used in the scenarios.

One final note – on the role of the observers. Too often this role is undervalued, if not by the trainer, then by the observing participants who are not acting in the role plays, and therefore feel 'off-the-hook'. Observers should be encouraged to use their assertiveness skills, 'listening' with eyes as well as ears to the interaction they are witnessing. When giving feedback, again, their own assertive approach can be practised, e.g. by taking ownership of their views and opinions, by giving positive feedback in a succinct and constructive manner, and so on. The observers' comments are crucial to the effectiveness of the learning as the 'actors' are sometimes more ready to accept criticism from peers than from the trainer. The trainer's role in the feedback session should be relatively minor, directing and guiding proceedings, ensuring that constructive feedback is offered, summarising the conclusions of the group and of the learning which has taken place.

Symbols

Handout sheet

Trainer's guidance

PART I

BROKEN RECORD

PART I

BROKEN RECORD

It is appropriate to start this manual with examples of the 'broken record' technique, which is central to assertiveness. Broken record means maintaining your stance and not becoming diverted, no matter what argument, persuasion or even moral blackmail is used to try and change your viewpoint. It *does not* mean repeating yourself like a parrot, using exactly the same words and phrases. It *does* mean using similar, equally clear and positive language until the other person understands and accepts that you are going to stick to your position.

It is a useful technique to acquire, since it can be adapted to most situations where an assertive position is called for. When using broken record, you should acknowledge that you have heard and understood the other person's viewpoint, while making it clear that your own position is firm. However, it should not, and cannot, be used rigidly to the exclusion of the feelings and needs of the other person. Often a mutually agreeable compromise can be offered so that a 'win/win' outcome is achieved which satisfies both parties.

Avoid over-justification – a succinct explanation of your viewpoint will often help the other person to accept it.

EXAMPLE DIALOGUE

'Brenda, I would prefer it if you didn't leave your briefcase open on the reception desk. There are papers and books everywhere; it looks untidy, and presents a poor image.'

'You agreed that during slack periods I could do some college work. I attend to client queries promptly – my reception work doesn't suffer. I need these manuals and notes to work from for my project – if I don't keep them in my briefcase, I'll forget to take them home.'

'I can understand that, but we need to keep the reception desk clear and tidy at all times. I'd prefer it if you didn't have your briefcase and all your notes on the desk.'

'But I need all these papers out – my project's got to be in by next Wednesday and, as you know, the case studies rely on real work situations. Mr Brown said it would be alright, and I really want to qualify well.'

'Like Mr Brown, in principle I've no objection to your working on your project when there are no clients to attend to, and yes, it makes sense to use your experience here for your case studies, but nevertheless, we have an image to maintain. The reception desk has to be kept tidy. Please keep your personal work and your briefcase out of sight, and keep the reception area clear.'

DO

- be clear in your own mind about your position, and in what way, if any, you are prepared to offer a workable compromise
- keep to your point, using clear, concise, unambiguous language, repeating key words until the other person understands and accepts your position
- acknowledge that you have heard and understood the other person's viewpoint
- use empathy, IF the situation and your position allow it
- give a brief explanation of your viewpoint, without over-justification or excuses, IF the situation and your position allow it
- remember that tone of voice, non-verbal communication and body language must match your choice of words. Maintain a neutral expression, good eye contact, and have a relaxed, open posture

DON'T

- repeat yourself parrot-fashion. Instead, using the same key words, rephrase your statement, adding empathy if appropriate. For example: 'I can't attend this evening ... I'm sorry; I can see you're disappointed, but I can't come with you.'
- get side-tracked or diverted from your position no matter what methods of persuasion are used against you
- show signs of impatience by your body language or tone of voice
- go 'over the top' with justifications for your position
- hesitate or show other signs of passive behaviour. The other person will pick up the signal that they can 'win' if only they persevere

1

Excuses, excuses

THE SCENE

All the staff at Bristows Worthing section have contracts to work from 9.00 a.m. to 5.00 p.m. with one hour for lunch. Pamela is an excellent worker and her boss, Rowan, agrees that if she ever left it would take two people to replace her. However, she has one fault. She is often between ten and 20 minutes' late arriving at work in the mornings. Because part of her job is to record staff absences, and to supply replacements where necessary, her telephone is ringing constantly from 9.00 a.m. when the switchboard puts the calls through to her desk. (Consultants and sales people have to report their sickness as soon as possible, and before 10.00 a.m. each day in order to arrange cover.)

When Pamela is late, Rowan or other members of the team have to leave their work and answer Pamela's telephone. Pamela's timekeeping is getting worse, so Rowan calls her into her office to discuss the problem.

ROLE PLAY: ROWAN AND PAMELA

Brief – Rowan

You don't want to upset Pamela and you do recognise that she works efficiently and well. In all other areas but timekeeping she is conscientious. However, as a manager you have to be fair to all your staff who are all at their desks by 9.00 a.m. each day. Your task is to obtain Pamela's agreement to be punctual.

Consider the problems caused by Pamela's lateness, and what you require of her. Know what you want the outcome to be. Anticipate how you are going to handle her excuses or explanations. Remember that you are practising the broken record technique.

Good luck!

ROLE PLAY: ROWAN AND PAMELA

Brief – Pamela

Rowan is going to talk to you about your timekeeping. She needs you to be at your desk by 9.00 a.m. each morning. It is your task to try to divert her from her objective by whatever means you can – give explanations for your lateness, give excuses, offer alternatives, get upset, or angry ...

Here are a few suggestions. Please use these only *if you cannot think of anything to keep the dialogue going.*

Blame the rail service. The only through-train you can catch barely arrives on time. If there is a delay for any reason, you are late. To catch an earlier, stopping, train you would have to get up an hour earlier.

Blame the nursery. You have to leave your child at a crèche before coming to work. If the nursery staff are late arriving, you can't very well just leave little Jamie on the doorstep, can you?

Explain that when you are late, you always make up the time by having a shortened lunch-break.

Complain that you do more work than anyone else anyway. What right has Rowan to criticize?

Suggest that if you're late, leave the telephone ringing, or let reception take messages which you'll pick up later.

ROLE PLAY: ROWAN AND PAMELA

Observer's brief

Read through *The Scene* trying to assess what problems Rowan is likely to face when confronting Pamela, and what points she needs to make, reiterate, and make yet again, until Pamela understands and accepts the situation. 'Rowan' has to remain assertive, while 'Pamela' has been given a brief requiring her to be as awkward as possible during the interaction, making excuses, offering alternatives, complaining and so on. Your task is to assess how well Rowan maintains the broken record technique in the face of Pamela's persuasiveness.

Read the following questions and keep them in mind while closely observing the interaction.

Rowan is effectively giving negative criticism. Did she temper this with any praise of Pamela?

Was Rowan specific in her criticism, or did she give a wandering preamble to what she needed to say?

Did Rowan become side-tracked by any of Pamela's arguments?

Did Rowan's tone of voice and body language indicate that she was in control of the situation at all times?

Did she repeat her statements or requests calmly until acknowledged and understood by Pamela?

Any other comments?

ROLE PLAY: ROWAN AND PAMELA

Trainer's notes

Rowan has three arguments with which Pamela cannot disagree:

1. Pamela has a contract to work from 9.00 a.m. each day. It is *her* problem, and no one else's, how she fulfills that contract, but fulfill it she must.
2. If other members of staff are at their desks by 9.00 a.m. it is unfair if Rowan allows Pamela to be the exception, no matter how good her work is.
3. If Pamela isn't at her desk to take sickness calls, *someone* has to answer the telephone. This means that their work is disrupted and put back by several minutes.

To process the role play, first ask Rowan if she was happy with the way the interaction went. With hindsight, what would she have done differently? Did she make any of the above points by way of explanation? If she justified her demands of Pamela in any other way, why did she feel this appropriate? Does she feel that, if this had been a 'real' situation, Pamela would now 'toe the line' and arrive at work on time?

Secondly, ask Pamela for her reaction to the role play. Did she think that Rowan treated her fairly? Did she leave the interaction feeling that there was a winner or a loser? What, if anything, could Rowan have done to make her more satisfied with the outcome of the exchange?

Finally, ask the observers for their comments, adding your advice to Rowan if appropriate.

2

The photocopier

THE SCENE

Bill is a sales rep for Kopikat photocopiers. On his last visit to Dickson's he persuaded Linda to install the new 'Kopikitten' machine, on a two-month trial basis. The 'Kitten' is a desk-top photocopier with many additional features, all contained within a small box. It is, as the brochure states, 'a technological breakthrough in miniaturization; a time-saving addition for any busy executive's desk'. Linda agreed to the terms of the trial – she would just pay for the copies used. If she liked the machine, she would keep it; if not it could be returned without obligation.

Linda *does not* like the 'Kitten'. Although the machine itself is compact, the accessories and paper needed take up too much room on her desk, as does the space needed for the throughput of copies generated. In principle, the little copier is a potential time-saver; for example, Linda can photocopy some letters received, scrawl a response on the original and return it to sender rather than dictate and type a reply, without having to leave her desk. However, the quality of the copies is poor compared with the larger copiers. Worst of all, for Linda, is that because the main photocopier is on the top floor of the building, her day is now constantly interrupted by others in her office and on lower floors of the building 'just dashing off a quick copy or two' on her machine.

The two-month trial period is nearly at an end. Linda decides to preempt Bill's visit by telephoning him to ask him to collect the 'Kitten' which she has decided not to keep.

ROLE PLAY: LINDA AND BILL

Brief – Linda

You like Bill, and understand that much of his work is commission based. He has been a supportive and helpful contact in the past.

Although, in principle, you like the idea of the miniature photocopier, and can still see some of its advantages, you do not, under any circumstances, want to keep the 'Kitten' on your desk. You want it removed from your office.

Your task is to plan a conversation with Bill which meets your objectives while recognizing his position. Use the broken record technique, and try not to be side-tracked from your purpose.

ROLE PLAY: LINDA AND BILL

Brief – Bill

You like Linda, and respect her as a colleague as well as a client. Nevertheless, it is vital to your position in Kopikat that you have success with the 'Kitten'. You need to have one installed in at least ten offices in your area to meet your quota. Linda does not want to keep the machine. It is your task to use every means possible to persuade her to install the 'Kitten' in her office.

If possible, use your own ideas to plan your strategy. However, if you are short of ideas, here are a few suggestions:

If Linda complains about the quality of the copies, suggest that she may not yet have learnt the correct balance of ink to toner, or have adjusted the print quality gauge properly. You offer to go through it again with her.

If necessary, admit that the internal mechanisms may need a slight adjustment. Again, you will come in and fix it.

Allow a 10 per cent reduction on rental for the first two years if she signs a contract. Even throw in a maintenance contract at a reduced rate if she agrees to 'sign on the dotted line'.

If Linda mentions the inconvenience to her, of other people using the copier, suggest that this is a management problem between her and her staff – the benefits of having a 'Kitten' far outweigh the problems involved. Or, of course, install additional 'Kittens' situated in different parts of the office. A discount could be arranged.

Play on Linda's friendship. Explain your dilemma; that you need to get the 'Kitten' installed in your best clients' offices so that you can constantly monitor and improve the product. Promise her the best possible personal service; continuous access to updates at reduced cost, etc.

If all else fails, try moral blackmail – you really need the commission; your job is at stake, and so on.

ROLE PLAY: LINDA AND BILL

Observer's brief

Read *The Scene* carefully. Linda's brief is to convince Bill that, under no circumstances, will she sign a contract for the 'Kitten' photocopier. She does not like it, and wants it removed from her office. While recognizing Bill's situation, she has to use the broken record technique until he understands and accepts her position. Bill's brief is to use every means at his disposal to persuade Linda to keep the machine. During the role play Bill may use his own tactics, but he has been given a few arguments which, if he uses them, could imply that a) Linda just doesn't understand how to use the machine (patronizing) or b) has a problem managing her staff (disparaging). It would be useful to look out for these comments to see how Linda handles them.

In addition, keep the following in mind while closely observing the interaction:

Does Linda give positive as well as negative feedback on the machine?

Does she explain succinctly why she does not want to keep the 'Kitten'?

Does Linda allow herself to become side-tracked by entering into discussion of issues such as discounts, or Bill's offers to come in to advise on the use of the photocopier?

Does she listen to, and empathize with Bill, letting him realize that she has heard and understood his point of view?

Did she repeat her statements calmly until accepted by Bill?

What did Linda do well in the interaction?

If you had been in her situation, is there anything you would have done differently?

Any other comments?

ROLE PLAY: LINDA AND BILL

Trainer's notes

Besides her ability to maintain her stance by using broken record, Linda may have been tested in other areas. Her competence *may* have been questioned by some of Bill's remarks, and issues such as 'women don't understand machines' may have been implied. If so, these too can be discussed through this role play.

Begin the processing by asking Linda for her opinion of how things went. Was she happy with her performance? If not, and with hindsight, how could things have been improved? Did Bill say anything which 'threw' her? If this had been a 'real' situation, would she have found it as easy to have maintained her position? If not, why not? Again, in a real life situation, would it have been easier to have had the meeting face to face? If so, why?

Next, ask Bill for his observations. Did he feel that he had been given a fair hearing? If he had been Linda, would there have been anything he would have done differently? If this had been a real situation, how would the interaction have affected their relationship?

Finally, using the questions asked in the Observer's brief if helpful, ask observers for their reaction, adding your own comments as appropriate.

PART II

SAYING 'NO'

PART II

SAYING 'NO'

If a request is made of us which we don't want to accept, and we refuse that request, we often feel guilty about our refusal: 'It wasn't much to ask'; 'I should have put myself out'; 'What will he think of me now?' These are the kinds of thoughts which go through our heads. However, if we agree to a request, when in fact we did not wish to comply, we tend to lose our self-respect, and our consent is at best grudging. We are in a 'Catch 22' situation, feeling bad about ourselves whatever our decision.

However, if the broken record technique is practised, and we keep in mind how our communication is going to be received by the other person – in other words, recognizing their needs while not losing sight of our own – saying 'No' becomes easier, and we feel increasingly comfortable with ourselves when refusing a request. It should be remembered that:

a) Assertiveness involves making decisions. There will be occasions when, however much of a chore it is, we choose to say 'Yes' when we would rather say 'No' (e.g. if an elderly relative asks you to stay just a little longer for a chat when you would prefer to be elsewhere). Saying 'No' *is not* having your own way all the time, or being in an 'I win, you lose' situation.

EXAMPLE DIALOGUE

'Joan, I really must go. I want to call at the florists before they close.'

'You and your flowers! Why not pick a few roses from my garden while I make another cup of tea? I don't have many visitors these days, and it's lovely having some company.'

'Alright Joan. Thanks. But I really *must* go after that. I'll have to be away by 5 o'clock at the latest. Agreed?'

b) Sometimes situations demand just a direct 'No', repeated until the other person gets the point. However, we don't ***have*** to refuse a request in blunt, unaccommodating terms. Admittedly, statements must be clear and concise, but they can be tempered with regret for the refusal (if this is genuine), acknowledgement of the other person's position, recognition of their feelings, and so on.

EXAMPLE DIALOGUE

'I'm really sorry I can't attend – I would have liked to be there – but on this occasion family must come first, so I have to say no.'

Or:

'I can see you're disappointed, but I have to refuse.'

c) Often, a workable compromise can be reached. This does not mean backing down, and it has to be acceptable to both parties. If the compromise offered is refused, however, it is important to return to the broken record technique – your original stance.

EXAMPLE DIALOGUE

'I can't be at the meeting on Friday – I've prior commitments – but I could go to the Dereby meeting next week, and present the paper there.'

'That's not good enough, I'm afraid. I want Mr Jones to hear that report, and he won't be at Dereby.'

'I'm sorry, but I can't change my arrangements to be at the meeting next week.'

Some general tips:

Listen carefully to what is being asked of you, with eyes as well as ears! Non-verbal communication can tell you a lot about the importance of the request to the other person, and may influence the way you respond.

Once the decision is 'No', don't be side-tracked by persuasive argument.

Recognize the difference between explanations and excuses.

DO

- remember your 'rights' – to decide for yourself what you agree to, and what requests you refuse
- remember that the other person has rights and feelings too. Recognize and acknowledge these needs while not losing sight of your own
- give a brief, succinct explanation of your standpoint IF the situation and your position allow it
- remember that it is also OK to say 'No' without giving a reason, and without feeling guilty
- make your decision to agree to or refuse a request based on how *you* feel, not on what is expected of you, or how the other person thinks you *should* feel
- use the broken record technique, offering a workable compromise if appropriate
- keep calm, using a firm tone of voice when saying 'No'
- remember to match your body language and non-verbal communication to the words you use

DON'T

- base your decision of what you should or should not agree to, on others' expectations of you
- say 'No' without hearing the other person out; they have the right to make a request of you (usually!). There may be occasions when a totally unreasonable request or demand is made, when a straight and forceful 'No' is the only possible response
- expect to be asked for a reason if you do not agree to the other person's request
- over-apologize, make excuses, or give lengthy explanations
- say 'No' in a way that appears hostile
- send out confusing signals, like smiling when you are forcefully saying 'No'
- think that because you have refused a request that this exempts you from asking for what you want in the future
- think that by refusing a request, the other person will cease to like you or find you trustworthy; will become angry, feel rejected etc. If handled assertively, you should both feel alright about the outcome

3

The gloomy corner

THE SCENE

Gavin has decided to rearrange the offices in an open-plan layout. This means taking down partition walls, moving desks and work stations and so on, in order to accommodate staff at present located in separate rooms. He has drawn up plans for the new-look office, and will present these to his team, for discussion, at the staff meeting this afternoon.

One corner of the room is quite dark because it has no windows – only swing doors to a corridor leading to other parts of the building. Because of this, it has had little use in the past, apart from storage space. Gavin's plan means using all available space for work stations. He has decided to locate all machines and machine operators in this corner of the office. There will be noise caused by word processors and printers to some degree, but the new arrangement will allow Paula, the typist, to feel more part of the team.

Paula is at present in a room on her own, separated from the general office. Through the grapevine, she has learned of Gavin's proposition, which means that she will be situated in the 'gloomy corner'. She finds this unacceptable because of lack of light and access to windows. Paula intends to say 'No' to the proposition at the meeting this afternoon. The role play will be between Paula and Gavin.

ROLE PLAY: PAULA AND GAVIN

Brief – Paula

You have only heard rumours about the proposed changes, but if they are true, you feel you have the right to refuse to work in unsuitable conditions. You are in a difficult position because it is your boss who will put forward the proposition which you intend to reject. (In 'the real world' it is often a manager senior to yourself to whom you need to say 'No', so this is good practice!)

In this role play, you have good reasons why it is impractical for you to be in that corner. Your task is to plan your approach, consider your key statements, and then use your skill to maintain your position, and not be pushed into something which is not acceptable to you. This may mean having to reach a *mutually agreeable*, working compromise.

By the end of the role play, you should have reached a point at which you feel good about both yourself and the outcome.

Good luck!

ROLE PLAY: PAULA AND GAVIN

Brief – Gavin

You have looked at the problem of accommodating all your staff within the one, open-plan room. To make it work, you *have* to make use of all available floor space for work stations – storage can be accommodated elsewhere.

Someone has to be in the 'gloomy corner'. It makes sense to isolate the essential machinery, such as the word processor, printer, franking machine, etc. in that corner, which means that, logically, Paula's desk will also be there.

Your task is to persuade Paula to agree to the move. One of the purposes of the open plan system is to encourage teamwork and commitment to the common purpose, so you don't want either to antagonize any of your staff, or to use your power, as manager, to insist.

Please use some of the following suggestions only *if you are short of arguments.*

Most of the other staff need constant access to the telephones, all of which are in the centre of the room.

The word processor screen has a brightness control which should help counteract the lack of natural light.

You could provide additional lighting in the form of angle poises, or uplighters.

ROLE PLAY: PAULA AND GAVIN

Variation

The role play can take place between just Gavin and Paula, or alternatively, the staff meeting could be acted out, with other members contributing to the discussion.

The latter alternative would add other dimensions: Is it easier to argue your case in a group with support from others? Is it more difficult to maintain a 'No' stance when pressure is from more than one person?

Optional brief

Other members of staff

One or two other training group members could volunteer to add authenticity to the meeting by putting their view of the 'gloomy corner' proposed allocation.

Possible arguments for Paula:

- eye-strain
- location of opening window

Against Paula:

- *someone* has to work there
- she must behave as part of the team
- should be grateful she wasn't just *told*
- chance to move out of her little, isolated room

ROLE PLAY: PAULA AND GAVIN

Observer's brief

Familiarize yourself with *The Scene*. Gavin's brief is to try to convince Paula that a move to the open-plan office system is a good one, but that in order for it to succeed, all floor space needs to be used, including the dark corner by the swing doors. He must persuade her that it is most appropriate for her work station to be positioned there. Paula's brief is to say a definite 'No' to the proposition, giving explanations etc. as necessary. She must maintain her stance unless a viable alternative is presented, with which (in the real world) she would be happy.

Watch the interaction carefully, and consider the following questions. You will be asked to report back to the main group after the role play has ended.

Did Gavin make a good case for situating Paula in the corner?

Did Paula listen carefully to his point of view before expressing her own opinion?

If not, what effect did this have on Gavin? If this had been a real situation, what conclusions would you draw from this stage of the role play?

Did Paula give clear and valid explanations for her point of view, or did she just protest and make excuses?

Did she speak calmly and clearly without becoming defensive or aggressive?

Did she use the broken record technique, repeating her statements until her position was accepted?

Did she acknowledge Gavin's point of view, while maintaining her own stance?

Did Gavin's body language betray what he was feeling?

Were Paula's tone of voice, facial expression, and body language consistent with what she was saying?

Did she look Gavin in the eye while she said 'No'? Did she apologize (or over-apologize) for stating her point of view?

What went well for Paula, and why?

What could Paula have done to improve her position?

(If the role play was conducted as a meeting with other staff members present):

Do you think it helped or hindered Paula, having to maintain a 'No' stance in front of colleagues?

Any other comments?

ROLE PLAY: PAULA AND GAVIN

Trainer's notes

Although this is a role play designed to test Paula's assertiveness in maintaining her 'No' stance unless a mutually agreeable alternative is offered, it also tests Gavin's ability to make a case and stand by it. This aspect of the role play could be discussed.

If both protagonists made a good case, or if a stalemate was reached, this again could be a good discussion point – i.e. what happens when two people, equally assertive, and equally adamant in their point of view, come into conflict?

To process the actual role play, first ask the 'actors' to describe their reactions, starting with Paula. Does she feel she has won? Lost? Did both she and Gavin lose, or did they both emerge having found a compromise? What did she feel she handled well? What, if anything would she have altered in her approach? Did she feel that she had kept in control throughout? Was she aware of things like her facial expression and her body language?

Next, get Gavin's views on how the role play went, asking similar questions to the ones above. Did he feel angry at any time? If this had been a real interaction, would he have been tempted to use the power of his position to *make* Paula agree? What did he feel was good about Paula's approach? If he had been in Paula's shoes, would he have done anything differently?

Finally, using the questions in the Observer's brief as a guide if useful, ask observers to give their comments on the role play, adding your own advice if appropriate.

4

The doormat

THE SCENE

Marjorie has worked in the same school as secretary for 12 years. Chris, the headteacher of the school, is a good boss, although Marjorie feels she is sometimes taken for granted. Marjorie is always willing to do anything for the children, staff and school, but on one or two occasions lately, without consultation, it has been accepted that she will do this or that to help out, in addition to her usual duties.

For the last three years, Marjorie has organized and run a Bring-and-Buy stall to raise money for the school. Although she didn't attend the last staff meeting, when typing up the minutes she read that the date for the next Bring-and-Buy had been arranged ... and that she was going to run it! She hadn't been asked; it was assumed that she would take the responsibility for it again this year.

Marjorie is more hurt than annoyed, and plans to speak to Chris about it – in fact to refuse – not out of spite, but because she genuinely cannot run it on the date arranged because of prior commitments. She is determined that, even if Chris suggests the date for the Bring-and-Buy be changed, she will not agree to organize it this year as a matter of principle.

ROLE PLAY: MARJORIE AND CHRIS

Brief – Marjorie

You have decided that, whatever Chris says, you will not organize and run the Bring-and-Buy sale this year. As it happens, the date coincides with your sister's wedding anniversary party, and you have already agreed to help with the catering for that.

Your task is to plan your approach carefully, and to initiate a meeting with Chris about the Bring-and-Buy, stating your case, and maintaining your position using the broken record technique.

ROLE PLAY: MARJORIE AND CHRIS

Brief – Chris

You accept that you assumed that Marjorie would organize the Bring-and-Buy again this year without first clearing it with her. Marjorie is going to refuse to do it. Your task is to persuade her to take on the responsibility again. Use flattery, persuasion, coercion – anything to obtain her agreement.

If possible, act out the role play using your *own methods of persuasion. If, however, you are lost for ideas, here are a few suggestions:*

Can't she arrange a different date for the anniversary party?

If she can't, couldn't she do the catering earlier and freeze the food? She would still be in time to attend her party in the evening.

Marjorie could leave early on the Friday before the anniversary to do the catering.

You could change the date of the Bring-and-Buy.

Nobody else has Marjorie's organizing abilities.

One of the teachers could run the stall on the day if Marjorie will agree to organize the event.

ROLE PLAY: MARJORIE AND CHRIS

Observer's brief

Please read *The Scene*. Marjorie has to practise her assertion, refusing to be involved with the Bring-and-Buy this year no matter how persuasive Chris is.

Observe the interaction between them, while considering the following points.

Did Marjorie state her case clearly, without a waffly preamble?

Did she give her explanations concisely, without too much padding?

Did her tone of voice and body language match what she was saying?

Did Marjorie allow herself to be side-tracked by any of Chris's arguments?

Did Marjorie keep to the task in hand – to make it clear that she would not be involved with the event this year – or did she confuse the issue with the other matter of being taken for granted?

Any other comments?

ROLE PLAY: MARJORIE AND CHRIS

Trainer's notes

There are two issues here. The immediate situation of Marjorie's involvement (or not) with the Bring-and-Buy event, and the long-standing problem of being taken for granted. Should the issues be handled separately, on different occasions, or should Marjorie take the bull by the horns and 'have it out' with Chris once and for all? The pros and cons of both approaches could be discussed with the group.

To process the role play, first ask Marjorie for her analysis of her performance. Was she happy with the way things went? If not, why not? What had she done well? If she had the chance to replay it, what would she have done differently? Did Chris do or say anything which she felt difficult to respond to assertively? Did she feel that she was losing control of the situation at any time? If this had been the real world, how, if at all, would the relationship have changed between Marjorie and Chris?

Next, ask Chris for her/his reactions. Did Marjorie acknowledge her/his position or feelings? Should she have done so in the circumstances? What might Marjorie have done or said to help her situation? What did she handle well?

Finally, work through the observer's comments, using their question sheet as a crib if this helps. Add any observations of your own.

5

Huggy bear

THE SCENE

Mrs Butler is headteacher of Prentis Junior School. Recently, there has been a spate of fighting in the playground, at breaks and at lunch-time. Some less-well-off children have been taunting the ones who brought their toys to school, often taking them and not giving them back, or even sometimes deliberately breaking them, largely because of jealousy thought Mrs Butler. Also, some children were being teased about their toys; others became aggressive because they wouldn't share, and so on. She decided that children's own toys were more trouble than they were worth, so in a letter to parents asked them not to allow their children to bring toys to school. The letter also informed the parents that toys brought to school would now be confiscated.

Dawn Bedford is the parent of a shy and timid little boy, Bruce. Dawn is annoyed and worried to receive Mrs Butler's letter, because, although Bruce is now seven years old, he still takes his teddy bear everywhere with him. It's his security; he's lost without it. In fact, when Dawn tried to wean him off it recently, refusing to let him take it on a visit to a friend of hers, he became quite ill. She is afraid that he will become school-phobic if not allowed to take his bear with him. Dawn has arranged a meeting with Mrs Butler to question the banning decision.

ROLE PLAY: MRS BUTLER AND DAWN BEDFORD

Brief – Mrs Butler

While you understand that the toys ban will be difficult for some parents to enforce, a rule is nevertheless a rule. You have to be fair, so there can be no exceptions.

Your task is to explain to Dawn Bedford why the answer to her question must be 'No', using all the techniques of broken record, including the offer of a compromise *if* you consider this to be appropriate.

ROLE PLAY: MRS BUTLER AND DAWN BEDFORD

Brief – Dawn Bedford

You understand that school rules are made for the good of all the pupils, but your main concern is for your son's well-being. Your task is to try to get Mrs Butler to agree to Bruce bringing his teddy bear to school.

Put yourself in Dawn's shoes, and act out the role play using your *own ideas and ploys. However, if you are short of ideas here are a few suggestions to get you started.*

Bruce has no father and is more insecure than most boys of his age. He needs his 'security blanket' – in this case, his teddy bear.

'You might *think* you know what's best for the children, but you don't know Bruce as well as I do.'

It won't be Mrs Butler who is woken up in the night when Bruce is frightened about going to school without his teddy!

It'll make Bruce ill, then he won't be able to go to school.

'He'll try to run home if he can't have his teddy with him. It'll be your fault if he gets lost or knocked down by a car.'

'I'm doing my best to wean him away from the bear. I want to be able to do things in my own time, at a pace that's right for Bruce, without your interference.'

ROLE PLAY: MRS BUTLER AND DAWN BEDFORD

Observer's brief

Please read *The Scene* carefully. Put yourself in the shoes of both women and try to assess their points of view. After the role play, you will be asked to give positive and constructive feedback to Mrs Butler – her brief is to assertively refuse Dawn Bedford's attempts to make her agree to make an exception in Bruce's case. Mrs Butler should use the procedures suggested in broken record.

While observing the interaction, please keep the following in mind:

Did Mrs Butler really listen to Dawn Bedford's argument? What evidence have you for this opinion?

Did Mrs Butler show empathy, acknowledging Dawn's point of view, while maintaining her own position?

Did she give explanations in clear concise terms?

Was her body language consistent with what she was saying?

Did she offer a compromise, or compromises, to Dawn?

Do you feel that, at the end of the exchange, the women had reached a mutually acceptable agreement?

Any other comments?

ROLE PLAY: MRS BUTLER AND DAWN BEDFORD

Trainer's notes

After the role play, process the interaction by asking the 'actors' how they felt it went. Begin with Mrs Butler.

Did she feel she had listened well to Dawn Bedford? What had she done to let Dawn know that she was listening, and had understood her point of view? Was she conscious, at all, of her own and Dawn's body language during the interaction? Did she feel, with hindsight, that the explanations she gave were adequate, specific, and given with strength of conviction? Was she happy with the compromise (if any) which was reached? What had she done well? If the role play were to be repeated, what, if anything, would she change in her approach?

Next, ask Dawn for her observations. Did she feel that she made her case, was listened to, and understood? Were her views taken into consideration by Mrs Butler? Could Mrs Butler have done anything else, or anything differently to help resolve the situation? If this had been a real discussion, how would she feel about the outcome?

Finally, ask the observers to add their comments, using the Observer's brief questions as prompts if this helps. Enquire whether they felt the compromises (if any) offered by Mrs Butler were appropriate, or whether, had they been her, they would have suggested alternative solutions. Ensure that constructive feedback has been given to Mrs Butler before closing the role play.

PART III

SETTING LIMITS

PART III

SETTING LIMITS

Setting limits is a similar technique to saying 'No', and can also involve broken record. It recognizes your own needs (as well as capabilities), taking ownership of your own uniqueness, and informing others of your own particular boundaries: 'I will go so far, and no further.' Setting limits enables the other person to know what you are prepared to do, and how you expect to be treated: 'I am quite happy being called by my first name, Susan; but I do not want to be called Sue or Susie.'

When you articulate your limits, you should remember that they do not have to be fixed in tablets of stone. Limits can change with circumstance, with different people, and in different situations. The Susan above may find it quite acceptable to be called Sue at home, with friends, but does not like the diminutive used at work.

There are other examples of how limits can be flexible. If you have a rush job on, you could inform your staff: 'I can't take any 'phone calls or interruptions for the next two hours, the exception being Jack Brown – please put his call through at once.' Here the limit has been set clearly for a two-hour duration. Or: 'Normally I would take on all of this gladly, but, because of family commitments, this year I will only be able to help in an advisory capacity.'

The important point is to recognize your needs and boundaries, and articulate your limits in a clear, unambiguous way.

DO

- remember that limits are individual. What feels comfortable for you, may not for someone else; what another person is prepared to do may not be acceptable for you
- recognize your own needs and boundaries which are independent of the demands of other people
- inform the other person of what you are prepared to do or how you expect to be treated in a clear, unambiguous way.
- be firm in your assertion, ensuring that all non-verbal signals match your words
- use the broken record technique if this is necessary, restating your position until it is understood and accepted
- remember that your limits can change with different situations, different people, and different circumstances

DON'T

- give excuses, or apologize for being true to yourself

6

The last straw

THE SCENE

Laura manages a busy public relations section of an international company. She has just been on a 'Managing Change' training course, and has returned to the office convinced that the answer to her problems is to delegate more. Laura's section is divided into three teams, one of which is headed by Beth. Although the other teams are busy, they don't seem too stretched. Beth's is working to capacity. She knows that at least one of her team is doing the work of two, because retiring staff have not been replaced. Beth is working flat out to keep her head above water, just managing to keep on top of the day-to-day running of her team.

Laura tells Beth that she would like to see her in her office. She has decided that there are areas of her work which would be more appropriate for Beth to undertake in future. For example, Laura would like to delegate the organization, staffing and running of the company's exhibition stand at Birmingham in six months' time.

Beth's natural reaction is to say 'OK' as usual, but her innermost self is crying out: 'I can't cope with any more – something has to be done.'

ROLE PLAY: BETH AND LAURA

Brief – Laura

You have never refused anything before. Somehow, you have managed to absorb all the extra work that recent redundancies and retirements have produced, but you cannot see a way of taking on any more. You have to make your position clear to Laura.

Remembering that you are acting out a role play on setting limits, use your own ideas to decide how you will develop it, if possible. Your task is to stand firm, or arrive at a mutually agreeable solution or compromise.

If you need some help to start, here are a few explanations or arguments you could use.

Your team can't take on more work without additional staff.

If you agree to help with or do the exhibition, then x, y, and z will have to be shelved.

Your team's work affects other areas – sales, distribution, and so on, so timing is crucial to you. Your work is seasonal, and must be completed by January and September to be in the stores for Easter and Christmas. The exhibition is in off-peak time for some teams, but not for yours.

If you take this on, some of your work will have to be done by other teams. Laura will have to arrange this.

ROLE PLAY: BETH AND LAURA

Brief – Laura

There have been huge cut-backs and redundancies throughout the company which has meant rethinking your own workload. The training course on 'Managing Change' has helped you think this through. You know that your plans will be met with resistance because it means a change of, or increase in duties for almost everyone in your section. You decide to speak to Beth first because a) she is less likely to disagree with your proposals, and b) it makes genuine sense for her to organise the exhibition. Your task is to try to get her to agree to the extra work, giving as little as possible in return.

Please use the suggestions below only *if you need ideas to start:*

You realize that in the past you organized and ran the exhibitions mainly because you *enjoyed* it rather than because it was appropriate to your position. It *should* have been Beth's responsibility.

Stress the benefits to Beth:

- status – representing company
- two weeks out of the office
- top hotel and all expenses
- direct contact with users and clients
- first-hand insight into the pros and cons of the product
- career development
- deserved rest after hard office work!

ROLE PLAY: BETH AND LAURA

Observer's brief

Please read *The Scene* carefully. To help with the role play, both Beth and Laura have been briefed with additional information. Please observe the interaction between them, keeping the following questions in mind. After the role play, you will be asked to give your comments on the exchange between Laura, who wants to off-load some of her work, and Beth who has to make Laura aware of her limits.

Did Beth state her case in clear, unequivocal terms?

Did she waffle, pussyfoot around issues, or give excuses rather than explanations?

Did Beth get swayed by any of Laura's arguments?

Did she empathise with Laura – did she, for example, state that she understood Laura's position, while standing firm on her own?

What did Beth's body language tell you about how she was feeling during the interaction?

Do you think compromises were offered, discussed and accepted as mutually agreeable solutions?

Any other comments?

ROLE PLAY: BETH AND LAURA

Trainer's notes

If Laura wished, as the boss she could always insist, of course, but Beth could equally inform Laura of the consequences to her other work if this course of action were to be taken. Setting limits, in this context, means demonstrating negotiating, as well as assertiveness skills: 'I'm prepared to bend on this, if you will give in on that.'

To process the role play, first ask Beth how well she felt she handled the situation. What did she find particularly difficult? Did any of Laura's persuasive tactics cause her problems? Were there any times when she felt she was being too passive, or in danger of getting aggressive? What went well? What might she have done differently?

Next, ask the participant who played Laura for her observations. If this had been a real world problem, how would she now feel about Laura? Does she feel that a mutually agreeable outcome was achieved? What did Beth do well? If she had been Beth, in this situation, what if anything would she have done differently?

Finally, ask the observers to give their comments, going through the questions on the Observer's brief if this helps.

It is especially difficult to role play setting limits, when insufficient detail is available on which to base arguments, so it is important for protagonists to follow this up with a role play based on their own work experience if possible.

7

The dependant

THE SCENE

Rose feels sorry for Paul. He is not a very bright lad, and is working a probationary six months with her as office junior. She has taken him under her wing, and covered up for him on numerous occasions when he has made mistakes. This has meant staying late after work to put right his errors when everyone else has gone home. She has tried to help him understand what is wrong, and how to correct the errors himself, but he becomes upset and anxious that he will lose his job. She put right some of his work, therefore, without his knowledge to protect his feelings.

Recently, however, Paul is also relying on her for support in his personal life. He lives with his elderly father, who apparently is not very supportive of his son. Paul asks Rose for her opinion on virtually everything before he makes a decision, and lately has also telephoned her home when he has a problem which he feels can't wait until the next working day.

Rose is beginning to resent this intrusion on her privacy. She decides that she has to speak to Paul about the situation, for his own good as well as her own. She suggests they lunch together so that she can 'set her limits', explaining to Paul what she is and is not prepared to do to help.

ROLE PLAY: ROSE AND PAUL

Brief – Rose

The last thing you want to do is hurt Paul, and you genuinely want to help him through his probationary period so that he can keep his job with your firm. However, work is work; Paul's other need for support is a different matter – especially as it is becoming invasive on your own spare time.

Your task is to decide what you feel is appropriate support for Paul, and to state your limits clearly. Paul should be left feeling good about himself, but in no doubt about the extent of your support in future.

ROLE PLAY: ROSE AND PAUL

Brief – Paul

Rose has to state her limits clearly, and keep to her intentions – to support you only within her prescribed boundaries. Your task in the role play is to use every means you can think of to divert her, dissuade her from her purpose, to back down, and even to apologize to you for bringing the subject up, if you can! Play on her good nature – sulk, be upset, hurt or annoyed. Try to make her feel guilty.

Ad lib the role play if you can. Only *if you are really lost for ideas use some of the following suggestions.*

'I have no friends apart from you; no-one else is interested in me.'

'I value your opinion on things. If I'm not sure what to do, you always put me right.'

'Without your help, I don't think I would have got through my probation at work. You're so patient, and never complain when I get things wrong.'

'You said I could ask your advice any time I wasn't sure what to do. I thought you meant I could telephone you in an emergency.'

'You're like everyone else – you say you want to help, but you don't really mean it!'

ROLE PLAY: ROSE AND PAUL

Observer's brief

Please familiarize yourself with *The Scene*. You will be asked to give your comments after the role play. Observe the interaction between Rose and Paul and judge how well Rose managed to keep to her task – of informing Paul, clearly and calmly, as to the limitations on the help and support she is prepared to give. Paul's brief is to do everything he can to make her back down.

Keep the following questions in mind.

Did Rose come straight to the point quickly, without unnecessary padding, or did she give a long-winded preamble to her statements of intent?

Did she look Paul in the eye while she spoke to him?

What did her body language tell you about the way she was feeling?

Did she speak clearly and calmly, using the broken record technique as necessary?

Did she get side-tracked, or become hesitant at any point?

What did Rose do or say which was particularly effective?

What, if anything, could she have done differently?

ROLE PLAY: ROSE AND PAUL

Trainer's notes

Rose is caught in the compassion trap. She is in a 'Catch 22' position in that she will become increasingly resentful of Paul if matters continue to escalate. She will feel she is letting him down if she is not 'there' for him when he needs support; but if she withdraws that support in an inappropriate way, she will feel guilty, uncaring, selfish, etc.

Process the activity by first asking the 'actors' how they feel the role play went. Begin with Rose; what did she think went well? Did Paul say anything to make her resolve waver? What was most difficult for her? With hindsight, what would she have done or said differently?

Next, ask Paul for his comments. Did he feel that Rose had shown an appropriate consideration for his feelings in her approach? What was good about the way she handled the exchange? If he had been in Rose's shoes, what would he have done differently?

To both Paul and Rose: 'If this had been a real office matter, do you feel that the outcome of the exchange would have been satisfactory for both parties?'

Finally, ask the observer's for their comments, going through the questions on the Observer's brief if this is helpful.

PART IV

ASKING FOR WHAT WE WANT

PART IV

ASKING FOR WHAT WE WANT

We all have a fundamental right to express our needs, and assertively to ask for, *not demand,* what we want. We must recognize, however, that we do not have a fundamental right to *get* what we want. We cannot always be in a 'win' situation, but at least by expressing our needs, our self-esteem is satisfied. Just giving in every time, or settling for something which is not satisfactory for us, just because we feel we haven't the right to make an assertive request, lowers our own self-respect, and ultimately loses us the respect of other people.

Some tips:

- know exactly what you want, not what you feel you *ought* to want or need
- be specific. Make positive statements (e.g. 'Would you do that outside please' rather than 'Don't do that in the kitchen.'
- Use 'I' statements rather than generalizations (e.g. 'I would prefer it if …'; 'I'd like you to …'; 'There's something I need to say,' etc.
- if you receive a negative response to your request, consider what you would be prepared to settle for, or, if the request is important to you, persist by using broken record in a calm, but firm manner
- remember your rights. You are entitled to state your needs, and ask for what you want without shame, and without feeling guilty

EXAMPLE DIALOGUE

'Have you decided on a colour scheme for the office yet, Pat?'

'Yes, I want Wedgwood blue walls, with white paintwork and a darker blue carpet.' (*A direct* 'I want' *statement.*)

'Oh, come on; you must be joking. Blue is far too cold a colour, and anyway, it's a bit masculine. Why not go for warm autumn shades, or pastels – they're far more you.' (*Not a direct refusal, but a put-down.*)

'I've considered the other options, Frank; I want the blues with white paintwork.' (*Brief response to relevant point, acknowledging that she has understood what Frank has said, but ignoring irrelevancies. Sticking to the point with an* 'I want' *statement.*)

'Well, how about keeping the idea of the dark blue carpet, but choosing a softer, more approachable colour scheme for the walls and paintwork?' (*Suggested compromise. Pat has to decide what she is prepared to settle for. If a compromise is acceptable – fine. If it isn't, she should persist until understood and taken seriously.*)

DO

- know exactly what it is you want, not what you *should* or *ought to* want or need
- communicate your request in positive, assertive language
- understand also what you *don't* want, and if appropriate, what you would be prepared to settle for
- make sure that you make your request to the appropriate person. It is manipulative to hope that a person learns of your need through the grapevine, i.e. by telling a third person in the hope that 'word will get around'.
- be specific. Ensure that your body language and tone of voice match your words
- Make 'I' statements; take ownership of your request
- probe further if your request is refused, listening carefully to the other person's point of view
- be persistent if necessary
- keep control over your emotions; and remember that asking does not necessarily mean getting

DON'T

- waffle
- demand
- hope that dropping hints will do the trick
- grumble about not getting what you want if you haven't articulated your request to the person concerned
- hold back for whatever reason from stating your want or need
- be put off if you don't receive the response you want. Probe, discuss, negotiate, or use Broken Record if the issue is crucial to you
- use other people as excuses for making a request that is important to you, unless, of course, you are legitimately representing others who share your view

Tg

8

Ear-muffs or showers?

THE SCENE

Astenn's is a small packaging company which makes its own paper, card and corrugated board. It manufactures presentation boxes and packaging for an exclusive market, dealing with just one or two leading manufacturing companies.

Because of a large new order, specialist equipment has been bought in. While this is efficient, and causes no problems in terms of workload, it is noisy, and creates more fine dust than the other machinery in the factory.

It is approaching the time for the annual review, when pay awards and bonuses are decided. Although, being a small factory, the staff do not have an official union, Don Settal has always met with the boss, Ted Astenn, about this time to put forward the views and needs of his colleagues in the factory. The staff have already had their meeting, and have decided that, in addition to a pay award in line with inflation, they require a rest room where they can take their breaks in peace and quiet away from the factory floor. (In the past they have either sat outside on the grass frontage in good weather, or used the neighbouring factory's canteen.) Also, because of the new equipment, they want:

a) the new machinery resited in a separate room, so that other machine operators can still hear the radio and tannoy
b) protective ear-muffs for the operatives of the new machine
c) showers installed in the washrooms because of the increased dust
d) better protective clothing plus free laundering of overalls

Don asked his team to prioritize their needs, so as to give him a better bargaining position. This they have done and, confident of the support of his team, Don calls a meeting with Ted to convey the staff's requests.

ROLE PLAY: DON AND TED

Brief – Don

Ted is a reasonable man, but you can't, in honesty, expect him to agree to all your proposals as they stand. However, your task is to state what you want, clearly and concisely, with the appropriate strength of feeling shown by your tone of voice, facial expression and body language.

At the meeting with all the staff, it was decided that your priorities were:

1. Ear protection for the operatives of the new machine. This is a health and safety matter; you believe the noise level exceeds that permitted without the use of ear-muffs, so you have the law on your side
2. The new machine re-sited
3. Showers installed
4. A full 8 per cent pay increase (will settle for a minimum of 4 per cent)
5. New and better overalls
6. Rest room
7. Laundering of overalls

You and your team are prepared to reduce your pay settlement *if necessary*. The laundering is not crucial. You are prepared to trade this year's bonus *only* if you have to, as long as the protective clothing and showers (at least one, but preferably three) are provided, and a separate staff rest room is agreed to. Your task is to arrive at a mutually acceptable agreement – a 'win/win' outcome.

ROLE PLAY: DON AND TED

Brief – Ted

Don will come to the meeting with a package of proposals. His task, as spokesperson for the staff, is to get as good a deal as possible. He will make several requests of you to which your responses should be various. Please put up as strong a resistance as would be reasonable if this were real life.

Use your own initiative in the playing out of this negotiation. To give you some idea of the possible range of responses to Don's requests, consider the following.

- agreement
- direct refusal
- compromise
- postponed, or deferred agreement
- excuses, but no refusal
- ignore request – change the subject – sidetrack the issue
- no response (e.g. say 'And what was your next point?')
- sarcasm
- put-down
- angry complaint – 'You're being unreasonable'
- aggressive verbal attack
- manipulation

Although you should make life difficult for Don, the aim is for you to reach a mutually acceptable agreement. This is what good negotiation should achieve – a 'win/win' outcome.

ROLE PLAY: DON AND TED

Observer's brief

Please familiarize yourself with *The Scene*. Don has a list of priorities. His task is to ask for what he and his team want, in a clear, concise and assertive way. Ted has to protect his firm's interests, and finances. It would not, perhaps, be reasonable to expect him to 'give in' to all Don's requests for additional resources.

Ted's brief is to put up as strong a resistance as would be reasonable if this were real life. He has been given some idea of the possible range of responses to Don's request. These are:

Use your own initiative in the playing out of this negotiation. To give you some idea of the possible range of responses to Don's requests, consider the following.

- agreement
- direct refusal
- compromise
- postponed, or deferred agreement
- excuses, but no refusal
- ignore request – change the subject – sidetrack the issue
- no response (e.g. say 'and what was your next point?')
- sarcasm
- put-down
- angry complaint – 'You're being unreasonable'
- aggressive verbal attack
- manipulation

Although you should make life difficult for Don, his aim is to reach a mutually acceptable agreement.

Please keep this in mind while observing the interaction. Some other questions to consider are:

Did Don acknowledge in his opening remarks that he understood Ted's position?

Did Don use appropriate assertiveness to talk about the staff's needs and the desired outcome without arousing defensiveness, or negativity?

Did he give sufficient by way of explanation? Did he go 'over the top' in justifying his needs? Was he ever long-winded or unclear?

Did Don listen well, and respond to Ted's arguments and objections in an appropriate way?

Did Don establish a 'win/win' climate? Did he show Ted how the improvements suggested might benefit his company? In other words, was Ted made to see what was in it for him?

Was Don's tone of voice, facial expression and body language compatible with what he was saying?

What did Don do well? What might he have done differently?

ROLE PLAY: DON AND TED

Trainer's notes

In this role play, Don was not only asking for what he wanted, but also representing others' needs, so it would have been inappropriate for him to speak for himself only, with 'I' statements. Nevertheless, he needed to be equally specific, brief and to the point, prepared to compromise over *some* issues – everything, in fact, associated with the concept of asking for what 'I' want.

Begin processing the role play by asking the 'actors' their views of the interaction. Did they feel threatened by it at any time? Were they comfortable in their roles? Did they feel they had both emerged with a 'win/win' outcome? What had Don handled well? At what point, if any, did Ted have 'the upper hand'? With hindsight, what might Don have done differently? How could the outcome have been different?

Next, ask the observers to give their comments on the exchange, using the Observer's brief questions if this helps.

Finally, issue a copy of Ted's brief to Don so that everyone has a copy of the list of possible responses to expect when making a request of someone. Stress that, where possible, it is a good idea to plan – have your facts ready, try to think as the other person will think, guess what their options are, and what their responses are likely to be.

9

Can I go?

THE SCENE

Meera has been Liz's deputy for three years, and over that time Liz has relied more and more on her support and advice. Not only has Meera her own responsibilities, but she can deputize in the fullest sense of the word, knowing Liz's job as well as she does her own.

Although Meera loves her work, and greatly values the comradeship and teamwork in Liz's section, she feels that the time has come to move on. She wants to apply for promotion, but needs Liz to back her. She knows Liz depends on her, and doesn't want to upset her. Meera wants Liz's approval as well as support.

ROLE PLAY: MEERA AND LIZ

Brief – Meera

You have every right to ask for what you want – in this case, the chance to develop your career. You need Liz to put you forward for promotion, and to give you good references. You know that she thinks highly of you, but fear that because she relies so heavily on you, Liz may be reluctant to agree to your move.

Your task is to use your assertiveness skills to state your case clearly and calmly, and while recognizing Liz's needs, maintain your own rights. The aim is to reach a mutually acceptable outcome if possible, but to uphold your position if not.

ROLE PLAY: MEERA AND LIZ

Brief – Liz

You feel a bit guilty because, although you have recognized that Meera has all the experience, skill and ability to hold down a more responsible position, you have never suggested she try for promotion. If you are honest, this is because she is too valuable an asset to you. This guilt is likely to make you behave more aggressively than the occasion demands.

You are also worried about how you are going to cope without Meera. The shock of realizing you might lose her, makes you recognize just how much of the workload she has carried. You are afraid to admit to yourself that she has excellent management potential, and is likely to rise higher in the organization than you might go. This too, affects your judgement of the situation.

Your task in this role play is to make life difficult for Meera, *for as long as is reasonable.* She has to maintain her position, assertively, in the face of your excuses and protests.
Please use the suggestions below only *if you are short of ideas.*

Make her feel guilty: 'How can you suggest moving now; you know I planned ... a long holiday ... or ... to go on those residential training modules ... or ... to take study leave. How can I leave the section with no deputy?'

Play on her friendship: 'I've never met a colleague with whom I've both worked really well and who I would choose as a friend. Surely working together is worth more than promotion? You may move on, but could be assigned to a department in which you're really miserable.'

Minimize her abilities: 'I don't believe you are ready for promotion yet. You haven't the staff management skills ... or ... sufficient experience in ...'

Try to postpone the inevitable: 'Maybe in a year's time I would feel able to put you forward, when we've had the chance to do another annual report ... or ... tri-annual projection ... or ...'

Make excuses, without agreeing or refusing: 'You've caught me at a bad time; I've got this report to finish for the meeting next week. Which reminds me – have you got the R&D stats yet?'

Give a direct refusal: 'No, I can't put you forward for promotion yet.'

Agree, but complain churlishly: 'Well, there's nothing I can do to stop you I suppose, if you're determined to leave me in the lurch like this. I do think it's selfish of you to go at our busiest time though. I thought better of you than that!'

ROLE PLAY: MEERA AND LIZ

Observer's brief

Please read through *The Scene* carefully. Meera's brief is to state what she wants clearly and assertively, and to stand firm in her intention to develop her career. Liz has to make Meera's task as difficult as possible. The following additional information about how she should play the role is given to Liz.

You feel a bit guilty because, although you have recognised that Meera has all the experience, skill and ability to hold down a more responsible position, you have never suggested she try for promotion. If you are honest, this is because she is too valuable an asset to you. This guilt is likely to make you behave more aggressively than the occasion demands.

You are also worried about how you are going to cope without Meera. The shock of realizing you might lose her, makes you recognize just how much of the workload she has carried. You are afraid to admit to yourself that she has excellent management potential, and is likely to rise higher in the organization than you might go. This too, affects your judgement of the situation.

Please keep this in mind while observing the interaction between Meera and Liz. After the role play, you will be asked to give Meera constructive feedback on her performance. Consider, too, the following questions:

How effective were Meera's opening statements? Did she waffle, or give a long-winded preamble to what she intended to say? Did she acknowledge her own feelings; explain that she was nervous, anxious; that she had mixed feelings about asking to leave the section, etc.?

Did Meera show empathy? Did she acknowledge Liz's feelings and needs while maintaining her own position?

Did she repeat her statements calmly and clearly until Liz understood and accepted her intent? Did she allow herself to get side-tracked? Did she stay in control of the situation throughout?

What did Meera's body language tell you about how she was feeling? Did she maintain good eye contact? Did her facial expression match her words? Did she show impatience at any time?

What went particularly well for Meera? What might she have done differently to achieve a more satisfactory result, or to have speeded up the process?

Any other comments?

ROLE PLAY: MEERA AND LIZ

Trainer's notes

Process the role play by first asking Meera for her observations on the interaction. Did she find it difficult to keep on target? Why? Which of Liz's objections or suggestions did she find most difficult to deal with? Why? What did she feel she handled well? If the role play were to be repeated, would she change her approach at all, or do anything differently? What has she learnt from the role play?

Next, ask Liz for her comments. Was she surprised by Meera's persistence (or lack of it)? Did she feel at any time that Liz was 'winning'? What did Meera do or say which was particularly effective? What might she have done differently?

Finally, ask the observers to give positive, constructive feedback, using the questions in the Observer's brief as a guide if this helps.

10

Statutory rights

THE SCENE

Tony runs his own small import/export business. Last month, he invested in technology to improve the efficient running of his business, and now has computer modem links with several companies and outlets around the country.

This morning, when he tried to exchange information with other firms, although the modem software appeared to be functioning properly, his computer failed to establish a telephone link with any of his contacts. Tony realized that the modem itself wasn't functioning. As it was still under warranty, Tony telephoned the firm who had supplied his computer and modem, to ask for an immediate replacement. The salesman with whom he had dealt previously has left the company, so Tony is put through to the assistant sales manager, Roger Block.

Note:
For those not familiar with the term, a modem is a device used to connect the computer to the public telephone network, and enables the computer to send or receive data from other computers situated in different geographical locations.

ROLE PLAY: TONY AND ROGER

Brief – Tony

Your task should be simple! You have three facts to aid you.

1. You have bought a modem from Roger's company in good faith, and have the invoice, receipt and guarantee as proof of purchase.
2. The modem is guaranteed for one year, and is still under warranty.
3. The modem is faulty – it is not functioning in the manner for which it was purchased – so it is your statutory right to receive a replacement or your money back

Your real difficulty is that you need a replacement at once – tomorrow at the latest. You know how to remove the faulty modem from your computer, and how to install a replacement.

Your task is to ask for what is, essentially, your right: replacement for faulty goods. Use all your assertiveness skills to achieve a successful outcome.

ROLE PLAY: TONY AND ROGER

Brief – Roger

Faulty goods are a nuisance to you. There is no financial gain in replacing stock – in fact, you lose money in real terms if the time taken dealing with the complaint, plus postage of returning goods to manufacturers, or repair costs are taken into account. You are therefore obstructive, rather than helpful. Although you know that the customer has basic rights in this matter, you try by every means possible *not* to replace or refund the faulty modem.
Use your own ideas to block Tony's attempts to get a replacement. If you want some arguments to help you start, here are a few.

Suggest that the modem probably isn't faulty; that the telecommunications firm probably had problems with the exchange when Tony tried to dial out. Ask Tony to 'try again later'.

Suggest that the modem probably isn't faulty. 'Have you checked that all the plugs are firmly connected into the computer and the telephone?'

Suggest that the modem isn't faulty. 'You probably made an error in your connecting sequence. Check with your manual and try keying in the information again.'

Explain that you can't give a replacement just like that. The modem will have to be returned to the manufacturers for checking. If it *is* faulty, then a replacement will be made directly by them.

Suggest that the modem is malfunctioning because of overheating. If the computer is 'on' all day, the modem can be adversely affected. 'Didn't you read that in your manual?' If this *is* the case, I'm afraid the damage won't be covered by the warranty.'

'OK, you bring it into our workshops here. We can't promise anything, but we'll check it over for you.'

'Of course we *would* replace it if we had one in stock. We would have to order one for you.'

ROLE PLAY: TONY AND ROGER

Observer's brief

Please read *The Scene* carefully. After the role play you will be asked to comment on the interaction between Tony and Roger.
Keep the following questions in mind.

Did Tony begin by asking for what he wanted in clear, unequivocal terms? Did he stick to the point, reiterating his requirements until heard and understood by Roger? Did he allow himself to get diverted?

Was there any point where it appeared Roger might be 'winning'? What (if anything) did he say which threw Tony, albeit temporarily? Did Tony keep control of the situation, and his own feelings?

Did Tony use 'I' statements throughout, or did he tend to generalize? Was he specific and to the point? Did he listen to what Roger said, acknowledge that he'd heard and understood, but stick to his position nevertheless?

Was Tony's tone of voice appropriate throughout? What are the pros and cons of face-to-face versus telephone interactions of this kind?

What did Tony do well? What might he have done differently to have produced a more satisfactory outcome?

Any other comments?

ROLE PLAY: TONY AND ROGER

Trainer's notes

Process the role play by first asking Tony for his comments on the exchange. Was he happy with the outcome? Did he feel that he had 'won', that Roger had 'won', or that they had arrived at a mutually satisfactory end result? What, if anything, had he found difficult? What went well for him? Why? With hindsight, what might he have done differently?

Next, ask Roger for his views. Did he find it easy or difficult to maintain his obstructive stance? Why? What did he feel was good about Tony's performance? If he had been in Tony's shoes, what, if anything, would he have done differently?

Finally, ask the observers for their opinion of the exchange. If it helps, go through the questions on the Observer's brief sheets. Ensure that the role play and processing concludes with positive constructive advice.

PART V

DEALING WITH THE TALKATIVE PERSON

PART V

DEALING WITH THE TALKATIVE PERSON

The difficulty in dealing with talkative people is in keeping your cool and remembering that more often than not, the person with whom you are communicating 'rabbits' for a reason. They may be lonely; may only see people to talk to occasionally; may have worries that they need to get off their chests; may talk incessantly out of anxiety. Of course, you will also meet the bombast, or the person who just likes the sound of their own voice. Whatever the reason, you need to treat the exchange with sensitivity, empathy if appropriate, and above all, patience.

The technique suggested here is similar to broken record in that you have to take and maintain the lead in the dialogue, repeating questions over and over if necessary, establishing and confirming facts, and keeping the other person on target. As with broken record, you must avoid being diverted. Keep the dialogue as objective as possible. Listen carefully to the spoken (and hidden) messages, and as soon as the other person's conversation starts to wander off the subject in hand, gently lead them back.

Acknowledge:

a) Their importance as unique individuals, by listening well. Maintain appropriate eye contact, use encouraging noises and so on.
b) That you have understood them by restating, e.g. 'so you're worried about this visit from your neighbour', or just telling them that you understand – 'Yes, I understand how that must have made you feel, so what did you do then?'
c) That you are interested, and prepared to help, by moving the conversation forward – '… I see, so you want a dress material to match these shoes? Do you want a plain or patterned fabric?'

EXAMPLE DIALOGUE

'Hello Mary, do sit down. I've heard about the theft of your handbag – I am sorry. I've got to fill in this report form for 'Security' so could you give me some details? Firstly ...'

'... well, I wouldn't have minded if it was my old handbag, you know, the one I usually bring in to work - the tapestry one. I bought that – oh let me see – must have been six or seven years ago when our Craig was tiny ...'

'So, it wasn't the tapestry handbag that was stolen. Can you describe the one which was taken?'

'Well, it was my Gucci one wasn't it? Well, not a genuine Gucci – they cost a fortune – but my friend Lena said you couldn't tell the difference, and it only cost ...'

'... so it was an imitation Gucci bag. Did it have the word 'Gucci' printed on it?'

'Yes, a sort of badge, just like the real thing, only I got mine at Batscombe market for only ...'

'And what colour was the bag, Mary?'

... and so on.

DO

- remember that there is often a reason for a person's talkativeness; they may be lonely, or anxious for example
- be patient but firm
- listen carefully; pick up key words which are relevant to the conversation and reiterate these to bring the person back on target
- take the lead in the conversation, continually bringing it back on course
- acknowledge that you have heard and understood by establishing and confirming facts. Move the conversation forward by asking questions
- maintain good eye contact; adopt positive body posture; make encouraging noises, and so on

DON'T

- show impatience or annoyance
- let the other person dominate the conversation; gently interrupt by re-stating what they have just said, then moving the conversation on
- get side-tracked. The talkative person will often also have a grasshopper mind, and before long you will be miles away from the subject of the original conversation
- cut off the other person's speech too abruptly though; treat the situation with care and sensitivity

11

If I only had time

THE SCENE

Mr Jones lives alone. He has been sold double glazing for his three-bedroomed house in Haysmere. He has agreed the price, signed the documents and paid his deposit for seven windows and a patio door. All that has to be decided now is: what sort of openings he wants for each window, i.e. side-hinged, or centrally pivotting (the price is the same); whether he wants the patio door to slide open from the left or right; and what kind of opaque glass he wants for the bathroom.

The surveyor, Mrs Bridges, is calling today to measure up and to clarify details with him.

She has been forewarned about Mr Jones. The salesman said:

'I was four hours with him. Could he make up his mind? First he only wanted the patio door; then just the windows in the back and front of the house; then just the patio again. First he wanted leaded lights ("But they would take so long to clean wouldn't they?") and so on and so on – and I got his family history thrown in for free!'

ROLE PLAY: MRS BRIDGES AND MR JONES

Brief – Mrs Bridges

You know from the salesman that Mr Jones is elderly, lives alone, and tends to waffle on. Although you sympathize, you are already running late and have three other appointments this afternoon.

You have to clarify what Mr Jones wants regarding the three outstanding matters, take accurate measurements for all the windows and doors ordered, check with Mr Jones that your drawings and measurements meet his requirements, and obtain his signature accordingly. You also have to arrange a date for the fitters to do the work – it will take them two full days.

Best of luck!

ROLE PLAY: MRS BRIDGES AND MR JONES

Brief – Mr Jones

Try to engage Mrs Bridges in small talk as often as possible. Try to 'hog' the conversation for as long as you can. Dither and prevaricate!

Please use the suggestions below only *if you are short of ideas.*

You are not sure whether you want side-hinged or central pivotting because of the draught factor (you suffer from all manner of ailments if you sit in a draught).

You are unsure about which way the patio door should open, because logically it should open on the left so that you can make the most of the sunshine in your back garden, but you are right-handed, so it would be easier if the right-hand door was the sliding one.

The *only* patterned glass you like is minimum obscurity.

You live alone. Since the double glazing salesman called, three days ago, the only person you have spoken to is the butcher.

You are concerned about, for example; your health; the fact that your daughter hasn't visited for months; the price of the double glazing re-payments; whether you should also have booked that summer holiday; etc., etc.

ROLE PLAY: MRS BRIDGES AND MR JONES

Observer's brief

Please familiarize yourself with *The Scene*, then read the following questions and keep them in mind while closely observing the interaction between Mr Jones, the talkative person, and Mrs Bridges who will attempt to complete a professional transaction with him in an assertive manner.

Did Mrs Bridges initiate an empathetic, but businesslike relationship with Mr Jones? How was this achieved/how could her approach have been improved?

Did her body language match her words/tone of voice? Did she show impatience? If so, how?

Did she allow herself to get side-tracked? Was this controlled, i.e. did she let him ramble on a bit and then bring him back to the point in hand, or was he 'cut off' too abruptly?

Did Mrs Bridges achieve all she set out to in the minimum of time while still listening to, and showing respect for, Mr Jones? How did she achieve this, or if she didn't, what could she have done to improve the communication between them?

Any other comments?

ROLE PLAY: MRS BRIDGES AND MR JONES

Trainer's notes

Firstly, ask the 'actors' for their reaction to the role play – how they think it went, whether Mrs Bridges felt she kept on track, how with hindsight she might have improved the communication. Ask Mr Jones whether he felt he had been listened to, and treated with respect, etc., and what evidence each has for their reaction/opinion.

Using the questions on the Observer's brief as a prompt, if this is helpful, get the reactions of those who watched the interaction, and match these with the views of the two principal players in the role play. If there are discrepancies, talk these through with the whole group, adding your own observations. Discuss what could have been done better, but concentrate on what went well.

Ensure that *positive, constructive* feedback is given, with the opportunity for the 'actors' to follow up this role play if possible.

12

By appointment only

THE SCENE

Richard was the first to admit that he was a disorganized manager. He didn't feel confident delegating, and consequently tried to do most things himself, which meant taking work home at evenings and weekends. He decided to go on a 'Time Management' course. As a result of this he returned to his office a new man. He instructed his secretary, Jo, so that he could make full use of her skills – she would monitor all calls from now on, keep his diary, and take over many of the tasks which would free Richard to concentrate on his managerial role, and make her working day more satisfying.

John is a sales rep, who does occasional business with Richard's firm. Because of a mutual interest in sport, John often calls in for a chat when he's in the area. They usually arrange to meet for a drink, or to go to a match, or play a game of squash. In the past Richard has been happy to see him, although he realized that John did most of the talking – once he began chatting about one of his favourite subjects, it was difficult to shut John up! However, it has been an excuse to relax for a while and think about something other than work, although Richard has been unhappy that John always stays for about an hour, no matter how busy he says he is. This inevitably means a mad rush to catch up afterwards, adding to Richard's already high stress level.

Richard has arranged with Jo that all meetings must now be diarized, by her, and that casual visits be phased out. However, when John next comes into the office, he breezes past Jo as usual, and before she can say anything he has established himself on the sofa in Richard's room. Richard tells Jo that it's OK; he will deal with it.

ROLE PLAY: RICHARD AND JOHN

Brief – Richard

You like John, enjoy his company and benefit from his friendship. He does chatter a lot, but the only person who won't take 'No' for an answer; arranges tickets for sports matches, or gives you a good game of squash – in other words, makes you do something other than work for a few hours.

However, you can't spare so much time out of your official working day for his impromptu visits.

Your task is to maintain your friendship, while making it clear to John that during working hours the relationship has to be strictly business.

ROLE PLAY: RICHARD AND JOHN

Brief – John

Richard has to make you realize that these impromptu visits have to stop. It is your task to chatter on, divert him, act hurt or offended – generally dissuade him from his purpose.

Please use the suggestions below only *if you are short of ideas.*

Begin the conversation with something like 'No sugar in mine today please, Richard; I'm on this new healthy eating programme'; or 'What are you doing this Saturday?'

Let Richard begin his explanation of how personal visits have to be curtailed, or whatever, then interrupt by saying that you *are* there on official business – you have a new product on which you'd like his opinion.

If Richard says you have to make an appointment with Jo, try to persuade him that, as you are there, and have the product with you, it would be sensible to talk about it now, etc.

Topics you could try to chat about:

- your new healthy eating plan
- the holiday you were thinking of booking
- the latest football/cricket/tennis match
- free to go to a 'stag' party on Saturday? Arrange to meet and how to get home later
- your friendship – how you value these chats

ROLE PLAY: RICHARD AND JOHN

Observer's brief

Please read *The scene* carefully. Richard's brief is to make it clear to John that these impromptu social visits have to stop, while ensuring that their friendship does not suffer. John's brief is to try his utmost to divert Richard from his task.

Keep the following questions in mind while observing the exchange between Richard and John.

Did Richard give John the opportunity to say whether his visit was business or pleasure before assuming the latter?

Were Richard's opening statements assertive – clear and to the point, while recognizing John's needs and feelings?

What did Richard do well in the interaction?

How successful were Richard's interrupting techniques?

If the exchange did not go well for Richard, how could his approach have been improved?

What did Richard and John's body language tell you about how they were feeling?

If this had been a *real* exchange, do you think that their friendship would be strengthened or weakened in the long term?

Any other comments?

ROLE PLAY: RICHARD AND JOHN

Trainer's notes

It is quite probable that Richard ploughed straight into explaining to John why he should first see Jo before coming in to see him, or why social matters should be kept to out of office hours, *without* first establishing whether or not John was on official business. If so, comment could be made on this.

Begin the process of discussing the role play by asking the 'actors' how they felt it went, beginning with Richard. Did he feel he handled the situation well? With hindsight, were there things which could have been improved? Was he surprised by anything John said or did? Did he feel he was losing the battle at any stage? Why was this?

Next, ask John whether he felt he had been treated fairly? Was there anything Richard could have done to improve things? If he had been in Richard's shoes, how would he have handled the situation?

Finally, ask the observers for their views, using the Observer's sheet as a crib if this helps. Ask if there are any further observations from anyone, adding any of your own as appropriate.

Ensure that constructive help is given. If possible, or if you think it necessary, allow the protagonists to follow up this role play, to practise any learning points gained.

DEALING WITH THE TALKATIVE PERSON

There is another type of talkative person whom we all recognize and have to deal with at some time or another. These are individuals who invade your time and try your patience; people who you cross the street to avoid – especially if you are in a hurry. These people just won't go away – will keep talking for ages – are only interested in their own point of view. They are poor listeners, so when you do get a word in, they will be eager to interrupt in order to continue their monologue.

Unfortunately, because of this tendency to dominate the conversation, they have few people with whom they can communicate on an adult-to-adult basis. Their interpersonal problems become increasingly acute, as more and more acquaintances avoid them. On the other hand, their need to talk increases, so the poor sould who does stop to chat to them will have a mammoth task to leave quickly.

In the working environment, 'talkers' of this kind cause a real problem. The situation has to be controlled or efficiency and productivity suffer.

Some tips:

a) Do be sensitive to their feelings. Listen well, don't show obvious impatience and don't be *too* abrupt.
b) Do not, however, let them dominate the conversation: preface your interruption with an acknowledgement that you have understood what they are saying. Then make your own statement: That's interesting – I see what you mean – but could I make the point here, that ...'; or, 'I can see that you are angry about that; could I say that ...'
c) If they try to interrupt before you have finished, try saying, calmly and evenly, 'Could I just finish what I want to say,' then continue. Use this, or similar, as broken record until you have impressed upon them the point that you require their undivided attention.
d) Don't say anything to diminish them as a person, but make it clear that, after a reasonable time, you *have* to go, so as to return to your work, or whatever. Again, firmly and assertively, insist on this using repetitive techniques as necessary.
e) Use body language to assist you. When you want to end the conversation, be the first to turn away. The movement need only be slight, but subconsciously it sends a message that the conversation is at an end and you want to be going.

If you are in your own office, stand up to greet your visitor – and remain standing, indicating that you intend this exchange to be a brief one. If the other person sits down, move around your desk and remain standing. This strongly reinforces your intention that they are not invited for a long stay.

13

Rabbit, rabbit

THE SCENE

Jane and Louise work for the same company, but in different departments. Jane's section is always very busy, whereas Louise's work is spasmodic. During slack periods, she often comes into Jane's office for a chat.

In the past Jane has unwittingly encouraged this, offering Louise a coffee – more out of politeness than as an invitation to stay. However, Louise makes herself at home and chatters endlessly about last evening's TV, her latest diet, problems with her neighbour, and so on. She doesn't want a conversation – just someone who will listen.

Jane has wanted to curtail these visits for some time – they have put her behind with her work – and is now conscious that her normally lenient boss is giving her warning scowls every time Louise arrives, although he hasn't said anything yet.

It's approaching lunch-time. Louise enters Jane's office announcing that she can't do any more to her work 'until Larry sends the invoices up this afternoon'.

ROLE PLAY: JANE AND LOUISE

Brief – Jane

You have three problems.

1. You are fed up with Louise's visits. You aren't interested in her prattle anyway; are annoyed that you can never get a word in edgeways; are anxious because your work is suffering.
2. You are concerned that your boss is developing a low opinion of you and might think that you are encouraging this time-wasting.
3. You feel guilty that you've not had the courage to confront this problem earlier, but feel obliged to do something now, although you feel sorry for Louise and don't want to offend her or hurt her feelings.

Your task is to have a conversation with Louise by the end of which you will have made clear your position and what you want to happen from here on, while being considerate of her needs and feelings.

ROLE PLAY: JANE AND LOUISE

Brief – Louise

You are bored with your job, partly because you have so much spare time on your hands. You are the only woman in your office, and the men are an unfriendly lot who obviously don't want to make small talk with you. Most of the women in other sections, although friendly in the past, now seem too preoccupied with their own work to want to stop for a chat occasionally. Thank goodness for Jane!

Please use the suggestions below only *if you are short of ideas. Try to dominate the conversation as much as possible, using every possible means to make Jane back down and agree to your continued meetings.*

You only pop in for a few minutes each day – it does Jane good to have a little break every now and then.

Your flatmate is on holiday. There is no-one at home to talk to.

You and Jane have so much in common.

There is a *no smoking* rule in your office; you need somewhere to go for a cigarette break.

Jane makes better coffee; in your section there is only cheap, instant coffee.

ROLE PLAY: JANE AND LOUISE

Observer's brief

Read *The Scene* carefully, trying to put yourself into the shoes of both Jane and Louise. Now read the following questions and keep them in mind while closely observing the interaction between Jane and Louise. Remember that Jane has to remain assertive in spite of Louise's attempts to hog the conversation, and to use all means at her disposal to get her own way.

How did Jane turn Louise's monologue into a purposeful discussion?

Did she give Louise any time for a chat, or did she launch straight into her own 'speech'?

How appropriate was Jane's timing regarding this?

Did Jane consider Louise's feelings? How was (or wasn't) this apparent?

Was Jane's body language and tone of voice consistent with what she was trying to say?

What did Louise's body language tell you about how she was feeling?

Was the outcome satisfactory to both parties, do you think? If not, what would you have done differently?

Any other comments?

ROLE PLAY: JANE AND LOUISE

Trainer's notes

Firstly, ask Jane how she felt the role play went. Was she happy with the way she handled it? With hindsight, what went well; what could she have done differently?

Next, ask Louise for her reaction. Did she feel she had a chance to put her point of view across? Was she listened to sympathetically? If she were *really* Louise, would she feel comfortable or unhappy about the discussion? What, if anything, could Jane have done to make her feel more satisfied with the interchange?

Now ask the observers for their views, using the Observer's brief as a prompt if this is helpful. Compare these 'outsiders' views with those of the 'actors'. Add any comments of your own which might be helpful. For example, if not already discussed, look at whether or not the interchange took place standing or sitting down, and the pros and cons of each approach. Discuss whether it would be appropriate for Jane to say something like, 'Look, I'm going to get into trouble with my boss if you don't stop dropping in for a chat' – should Jane lay the blame at someone else's door, or make assertive 'I' statements, taking responsibility for her own actions? Should Jane tackle the issue of the impromptu visits *and* Louise's annoying habit of hogging the conversation at the same meeting? If not, what should be her priority?

Allow 'actors' to follow up this role play if possible.

PART VI

DEALING WITH THE ANGRY PERSON

PART VI

DEALING WITH THE ANGRY PERSON

Consider times when you have been very angry. If the person you are annoyed with responds with 'You *are* in a state – now calm down', or, 'Don't you bloody well shout at me!', what would be your reaction? Quite probably, your anger would escalate by a couple of notches at least. By patronizing, or by meeting anger with anger, all that is achieved is at best stalemate, and at worse an explosive situation where rational conversation becomes impossible.

When confronted with an angry person you first have to accept that anger is a legitimate human emotion – one which many of us find difficult to express. Because of conditioning, we often repress it, doing no good to ourselves. Therefore, when a person does forcibly express anger, we must assume that there is a valid reason for that anger. We should also recognize that some people are more volatile than others, some have less self-control, and some respond more to 'gut reaction' than to logic. All need appropriate handling.

How you cope with a person's anger does depend (it must be admitted) on whether it is a personal matter, or one which affects your working life. In the former, if all else fails, you can walk away from the situation; in the latter, other elements are in play – customer care, or the need to keep your job, for example. The anger must be managed, and the customer, client, or boss pacified.

Some tips:

- realize that the angry person needs to let off steam. Provided that this is not too disruptive, a little time should be allowed for this. Listen well for what is being said. Let them know that you have heard them accurately and have taken in what they're saying. Observe well for hidden messages.
- without being aggressive, respond with a firm approach, and a direct facial expression. Maintain a calm stance
- attract the person's attention. A repetition of their name is a good

way of doing this. Once they are looking at you, maintain eye contact, and follow through immediately with a short statement, showing that you recognize and acknowledge their anger: 'You're obviously very annoyed; what exactly went wrong?'; 'I can see how angry you are. Have I got it right; this is the second time that ...?'

- empathise: 'I can see why that made you furious.' You are acknowledging their point of view; but in a business situation when dealing with an angry customer or client, it is important that you don't *agree* with them that 'the administration is a shambles' or 'the sales reps are morons' or 'the goods are shoddy'. Professionalism and loyalty to the firm must be paramount – even if you sympathize with the complainant!
- keeping a calm, even tone and level of voice, establish the facts: 'so the second batch delivered had the same mechanical defects ... do you have the code numbers with you?'
- if appropriate, apologize once and sincerely for any error or misunderstanding which caused the angry outburst, 'I can see why you're angry; I'm sorry, that shouldn't have happened ... then set about putting things right: ... 'I'll 'phone our distribution section now, and get an alternative widget sent to you with your next consignment.'
- repeat your statement of intent, using the person's name, until they calm down. 'I'll just 'phone distribution for you Mr Smith ...'. It may be possible to offer an alternative: 'Would you like me to make an appointment for you with our Head of Customer Services?'
- ask if anything further can be done to improve things. If Mr Smith has any suggestions, employ active listening to check facts. Affirm that you have heard and understood.

DO

- stay calm
- allow the other person some time to 'let off steam'
- listen well and let the other person know that you have heard and understood
- acknowledge their anger; empathize if appropriate
- try to establish the cause of their anger, and do what you can to establish a solution/workable relationship/compromise/positive outcome
- remember that you have the right to be treated with respect, and not to be threatened
- help the other person to behave assertively by your own example
- maintain a neutral posture, facial expression and tone of voice. Keep steady eye contact
- remember your right not to assert yourself. A passive or more aggressive stance may be necessary to make some situations work for, rather than against you

DON'T

- go into immediate 'fight' or 'flight' mode. Keep calm and assess the situation
- allow the other person to intimidate you. You must work towards a solution where at least your self-esteem is intact
- be tempted to join in, and become angry and aggressive too. Work towards mutual understanding and a positive outcome to the conversation
- let your body language give you away. Maintain an assertive stance
- be dismissive of the other person's anger. This will probably escalate the problem

14

Piggy-in-the-middle

THE SCENE

Sally heads the sales administration section of a fashion company. She had been aware that, because of the recession, sales for the year had fallen, and top management had been considering ways of retrenching. She asked her boss what the current position was. He told her that it was proposed to close the offices where her department works, and to relocate in a building next to the factory, at present housing the finance and personnel departments. The factory isn't far away – about five miles out of town – so shouldn't present problems for those staff who agree to the move. When Sally pressed him on the question of possible redundancies, he wouldn't commit himself, saying that he hoped natural wastage would cover any essential job losses. 'There will be a meeting of all section heads next Wednesday,' he said. 'The MD will give you all the official information then.'

Sally is aware that her staff have also heard rumours, and are feeling unsettled. She decides to hold a meeting straight away to let people know the present situation, and to reassure them that she will report in full on next Wednesday's meeting. However, before she can arrange this meeting, Bob – a fiery member of her team – barges into Sally's office demanding to know, 'What the hell's going on?'

ROLE PLAY: SALLY AND BOB

Brief – Sally

You too feel threatened, and annoyed that as a manager of staff, you have not been kept informed of proposed changes.

Bob is a good worker, but prone to fly off the handle at the least thing. When it comes to big issues – like this one – you had anticipated that he would be hostile and angry. You now have to use your skills, as a manager, to handle the situation appropriately.

ROLE PLAY: SALLY AND BOB

Brief – Bob

You are known to have a fiery temper, and on this occasion you feel that you are justifiably angry, and have a right to tell management – and that includes Sally – just what you think of them! You have taken it upon yourself to be spokesperson for your colleagues. You want some answers, and you want them now.

Sally's brief is to respond to your anger assertively, remaining calm and rational. Your brief is to maintain your anger as long as you feel reasonable, using every ploy you can think of to break her calm or professionalism.

Anger is essentially a spontaneous emotion, so you will have to ad lib the scene. If this proves difficult, here are some suggestions to help you.

She *must* have known what was going on before now – after all, she is management isn't she?

You already travel in to the office from outside town. This move will add at least an hour to your travelling time. There's no way you'll be able to do that.

Why hadn't anyone been consulted about any proposed changes?

It's alright for her – she's management – but the other building won't accommodate everyone. Who'll be made redundant?

ROLE PLAY: SALLY AND BOB

Observer's brief

Please read *The Scene* carefully. Sally has to maintain a professional stance while defusing Bob's anger. Her brief is to stay calm and firm in the face of Bob's outburst. Bob has been instructed to stay angry for as long as is reasonable, using every means possible to 'rattle' Sally.

Please observe the interaction between them, keeping in mind the following points about which you will be asked to report at the end of the role play.

Did the protagonists act out the meeting sitting or standing? In a real situation, would this have made a difference? If so, in what way?

Did Sally stay professional throughout? Did she associate herself with her team? If so, in what way? Was this appropriate in the given situation? Did she ever lay the blame for the current unease on top management? Should she have done?

Did Sally remain calm and rational throughout? Did her tone of voice and body language match her words?

What methods did Sally use to manage Bob's anger? What went well? What could Sally have done better?

Any other comments?

ROLE PLAY: SALLY AND BOB

Trainer's notes

Begin by asking Sally whether she was pleased with the way she handled the situation. Did she feel in control, and that she had placated Bob? With hindsight, what would she have changed? Did anything about the interaction surprise her?

For example, often, naming your perception of the situation (e.g. 'I see you feel very strongly about this'; or 'You're obviously really angry') provides an instant antidote. You've implied 'It's alright. I understand you're mad'. You've already begun to dissipate the aggression, and started to talk about what the anger is about.

Another aspect which surprises some people is that, having empathised with an angry person, perhaps apologized and suggested a solution, their anger is suddenly deflated, and you are left with a silence. The advice here is, follow up at once to maintain your advantage before the other person gets a second wind!

Next, ask Bob for his observations of the role play. Did he feel that he had been listened to, and that his real fears had been understood? What had (or hadn't) Sally done to achieve this?

Did he find it easy or difficult to stay angry? Why?

What did Sally do or say that was particularly effective?

If he had been Sally, would he have handled the situation differently? How?

Finally, ask the observers to add their views on the role play, going through the questions on the Observer's sheet if this is helpful.

Add your own observations if appropriate, ensuring that the role play session ends with positive, constructive feedback.

15

Pay up or ...

THE SCENE

Evans and Son is a small business. They have been suppliers of building materials – hardware such as nails, bolts and screws, plus tools and accessories – for three generations. They have always operated on a system of trust with local builders, and until lately had given three months' credit to all as a matter of course. Because of the unstable nature of building work, this three months had often been extended by old Mr Evans. 'They'll give me my money as soon as they get theirs' had been his motto.

Last month, old Mr Evans died, and David – the 'Son' in Evans and Son – took over. The business is not in a healthy position – in fact, there is a serious cash-flow problem – so one of the measures that David decided to take was to stop all credit. 'From now on, everyone pays for everything up-front' he told his storeman. 'Very large orders we'll invoice, of course, but interest will be charged on accounts not settled within seven days. I'll write to our regulars to that effect.'

The letter reads as follows:

> Dear
>
> CREDIT FACILITIES
>
> This is to inform you that it has become necessary to change credit arrangements. From the end of this month, all credit for goods will cease; payment for items across the counter should be made in cash, by cheque, or by banker's order.
>
> Obviously, for your convenience, we will invoice for very large orders. These invoices will be sent at the end of each month, payment to be made within seven calendar days. Interest will be charged on accounts not settled within this time.

We regret that these changes have to be made, and hope you understand the necessity of this decision.

Yours sincerely

David Evans

George Atkins, a local carpenter, had always dealt with Evans and Son. He was both worried and outraged by the letter. While still fuming about the letter's implications, he decides to go straight to Evans and Son and confront David with it.

ROLE PLAY: DAVID AND GEORGE

Brief – David

George is outraged by the letter he has just received.

a) He is unaware that anyone else has received a similar letter.
b) He is worried about the implications for his own business.

It is your task to defuse George's anger and to make him understand your position.

ROLE PLAY: DAVID AND GEORGE

Brief – George

You are very angry about the tone of the letter. You see no reason why your credit should be stopped. If it is stopped, your own business will suffer. In the role play, maintain your anger and outrage for as long as is reasonable.

Use the suggestions below only *if you are lost for ideas.*

How dare he write to you in this manner – you have always settled your debts and never abused Evans's credit arrangements

Old Mr Evans would turn in his grave if he knew what David was doing to his company.

Our two families have been friends for years – it's an insult to that friendship to imply that my credit is not good.

Closing down credit arrangements will cripple small businesses in the area.

How can I accept a big job, for which I won't be paid for months, if I can't buy materials on tick? My cash flow won't run to it.

If I can't have credit from you, I might as well go for the discount offered at the big D.I.Y. houses.

ROLE PLAY: DAVID AND GEORGE

Observer's brief

Please read *The Scene* through carefully; then look at David Evans's letter. Obviously, he has not handled the situation well, and one suspects that George's will be the first of many visits, letters, and telephone calls he will have to deal with. David has to dissipate George's anger, and while explaining his own position, reach some compromise if both his own and George's businesses are to survive. George's brief is to maintain his outrage for as long as is reasonable to test David's powers of assertiveness in the face of (justifiable) anger.

Please read the following questions and keep them in mind while closely observing the interaction between David and George.

Did David *actively* listen to George?

Did David initially defend himself, or retaliate? If so, what effect did this have on George?

What did David handle well in the interaction?

If you had been in David's position, what would you have done differently?

Was the outcome of the interaction satisfactory to both parties, do you think?

Any other comments?

ROLE PLAY: DAVID AND GEORGE

Trainer's notes

This is a role play where a person has to cope assertively in the face of justifiable anger. In real life, an explanation and a compromise are called for, as well as an effective handling of the angry outburst. The issue of effective written communication can, if appropriate, also be discussed during the processing of the role play.

To process the activity, ask the 'actors' how they felt the exchange progressed, beginning with David. Did he feel he handled the situation well? What, if anything, did George's tone of voice, and body language tell him about how the interaction was progressing? With hindsight, how might he have improved on the meeting with George?

Next, ask George for his comments. Did he feel he had been listened to and treated with empathy and respect? What did David do to handle his anger? Was he successful? Was there anything he did which didn't help, or even made matters worse? If he had been David, how would he have handled the situation?

Finally, ask the observers for their comments, using the questions on the Observer's sheet as a prompt if this helps. Ask observers what evidence they have for their opinions.

If possible, allow the 'actors' to follow up this role play, preferably with a situation relevant to their own work.

16

Hot stuff

THE SCENE

Marcus Panelli manages the restaurants and bars at the Grange Hotel. He has a first-class staff but, because of an outbreak of flu, he has had to employ both chefs and waiting staff to cover absences through sickness.

Ben and Sarah have ordered their meals. The service is not as good as usual – there are long delays – but the food is always good, so they have not complained. When the main course arrives, Sarah adds her vegetables to her plate before cutting into the Chicken Kiev. The garlic butter has barely melted, and the chicken is pink and raw inside. She calls the waiter across and says, 'This chicken is raw. Please take it away and cook it properly.' The waiter takes her at her word and returns, five minutes later, with the same chicken piece which has been returned to the deep-frier. There is now no evidence of the garlic butter, and the chicken is very dark brown on the outside and tough and crisp looking on the inside – hardly the succulent Chicken Kiev she had ordered!

Ben has by now almost finished his main course. He calls the waiter. 'Please go and fetch a new, properly cooked Chicken Kiev; this one's inedible.'

Some 15 minutes later, a plump, appetizing Chicken Kiev arrives at their table – but on the original plate complete with the (by now cold and congealed) vegetables.

Ben's anger explodes! 'I want to see the manager – *now*!,' he shouts. The waiter scuttles off, and almost immediately returns with Mr Panelli.

ROLE PLAY: MARCUS AND BEN (OPTIONAL SARAH)

Brief – Marcus

You do not know why you have been summoned to the restaurant; just that there is a very irate customer who wants to see you.

Your task is to manage the matter appropriately, and arrive at a mutually agreeable outcome.

ROLE PLAY: MARCUS AND BEN (OPTIONAL SARAH)

Brief – Ben (and Sarah)

You feel you are justifiably angry. The service has been slow, and the results, so far as Sarah is concerned, appalling. Ben's food had been good, but his enjoyment spoilt both by the situation regarding Sarah's meal, and the fact that he had to eat alone – finishing his main course before Sarah's order had been sorted out (which it never had been, satisfactorily).

Your brief is to verbally attack Marcus, 'with all guns blazing'. Please remain angry for as long as you consider reasonable, and until you feel that a satisfactory conclusion has been reached. You should find no difficulty thinking of things to say to Marcus about the quality of service in his restaurant, but if you are short of ideas, here are a few suggestions.
Take issue with the:

- delays experienced
- indifference of his staff
- scruffy presentation of food

You could suggest that:

- you will never eat in his establishment again
- you will warn everyone waiting in the bar about the poor quality of service
- you will tell all your acquaintances
- your company will boycott all hotels in the chain in future
- you will write to the local press

ROLE PLAY: MARCUS AND BEN (OPTIONAL SARAH)

Observer's brief

Please familiarize yourself with *The Scene*.

Consider the following questions while carefully observing the role play between Marcus and Ben (and Sarah).

Where did the interaction take place? Did Marcus conduct the exchange 'at the table' or, in the role play, did he ask Ben and Sarah to go with him to his office?

Did Marcus allow Ben to 'let off steam' before trying to give his own explanations of the situation?

Did he empathize with the couple? How did he do this? Did he establish the facts of the situation? How did he do this?

Did Marcus ever make excuses, or did he offer explanations in a calm and rational way?

Did he apologize *appropriately* for the situation?

What did Marcus's body language tell you about how he was feeling at the various stages of the interaction?

What did Marcus do well?

How could his approach to the problem have been improved?

Any other comments?

ROLE PLAY: MARCUS AND BEN (OPTIONAL SARAH)

Trainer's notes

This is a situation where, in business, 'the customer is always right'. In this case the customer *is* right, and is justifiably angry.

Firstly, ask Marcus for his opinion of the role play. Did he find it easy or difficult to placate Ben? Why? What was he pleased about in his own performance? What could he have done better? If this had been real life, does he think that Ben and Sarah would give his restaurant another chance and frequent it again?

Next, ask Ben (and Sarah) for his (their) comments. Did Marcus handle the situation well? What was especially good? What could he have done better, or differently? If this had been real life, would you have been happy with the outcome? Why?

Finally, ask for observer comments, going through the questions on the Observer's brief if this helps, and adding any additional advice if appropriate.

PART VII

HANDLING YOUR OWN ANGER

PART VII

HANDLING YOUR OWN ANGER

Why is it that so many of us can demonstrate anger – by sarcasm, or sulking, or lashing out, or swearing – but find it difficult to simply admit to and name that anger. It surely is true that, just by saying, 'I am angry about …' the anger and aggression will begin to diminish. Then we are on the way to discussing what it is, specifically, that is causing the anger.

There are other people who, because of conditioning (being told from childhood that it is unseemly to show anger, or that losing your temper demonstrates a lack of control) repress anger, thus denying the body the release of the stress and tension that anger brings. Again, if the anger is articulated, and the source of anger confronted, the process of calming down and resolving matters has begun.

When expressing anger, tone of voice is important; it should carry the weight of your conviction, volume and force increasing until the recipient gets the message. Appropriate body language and facial expression are also vital. For example, if you stand, feet apart, hands on hips, head poking forward, your words could be construed as aggressive rather than assertive. Or if your words are forceful, but you say them with a smile on your face, the recipient will be getting mixed messages about the seriousness of your assertion.

EXAMPLE DIALOGUE

If anger is acknowledged and acted upon immediately and assertively (rather than dropping hints, or expecting the other person to know instinctively that you're annoyed) there is more chance of a quick, amicable outcome. You will be less likely to attack the situation with a sledgehammer when a feather would have done!

Calmly, but with appropriate tone and volume:

'Rosie, this is the second time I've asked you to clear away your things and go to bed. I'm angry now; do it at once.'

'But Mum, I've only got two spaces to go and I'll have beaten the Spacerunner.'

Move up a gear; increase volume and strength of delivery:

'Please do as I say *right now*, and go to bed.'

'Oh Mum' [whining] 'just a couple more minutes and …'

Up another gear, giving an ultimatum:

'I'm really angry. If you don't do what I ask, right now, you will be grounded for a week.'

DO

- remember that it is difficult for most people to express negative feelings in an appropriate way
- give yourself permission to feel and express anger
- recognize that by stating your anger – 'I am really angry about ...' you are opening a discussion of why you feel angry. Discussion is more constructive than confrontation
- use 'I' messages – 'I resent it when ...' rather than 'You' messages – 'You really annoy me when you ...'
- use a tone of voice which is appropriate to the situation, and carries the weight of your conviction
- match the intensity of your response to the demands of the situation
- maintain an open assertive body stance. If your body is bristling, taut and 'aggressive', your words will be construed as aggressive too
- maintain good eye contact

DON'T

- stifle your anger. Repressing negative emotions is bad for the health, and ultimately for interpersonal relationships
- understate your feelings
- smile. This is tantamount to apologising for your anger
- over-react. Keep control of your emotions

17

Who's in charge?

THE SCENE

Denise has recently been promoted, and has taken over from Bob as head of a small department. Bob has also been promoted, and now heads the marketing section situated just across the corridor from Denise's office. While Denise admits that she has a lot to learn about her new job, she is incensed that one of her staff, Philip, still goes to Bob with any query or problem, or when a management decision has to be taken. On one or two occasions she has asked Philip why he has followed a particular course of action, to be told that, 'Bob said it was OK' or, 'I asked Bob, and he said to …'. Because of her inexperience with the work of the section, and the fact that she didn't want to upset relationships with her new staff, Denise has let it pass, just suggesting, that in future, if Philip has a query or problem he is to come to her with it. This has been ignored.

This morning, the situation has come to a head. Denise has received an irate telephone call from a client who insisted he speak with the head of section. Philip had made a serious blunder over an order, about which Denise knew nothing. She was made to look an incompetent fool with the client. On questioning Philip, he said, predictably, 'Well I wasn't sure, so I asked Bob about it – he told me to …'

Denise is understandably extremely angry. She decides to speak firstly to Philip, and then to Bob about the situation.

Role plays:

Denise and Philip
or
Denise and Bob

ROLE PLAY: DENISE, PHILIP, BOB

Brief – Denise

You must resolve matters once and for all if you are to maintain credibility in your section.

Your task is to leave both Philip and Bob in no doubt about how you feel, and what you expect of them in the future.

ROLE PLAY: DENISE, PHILIP, BOB

Brief – Philip

Your task is to offer as many reasons, explanations, and excuses as possible, to try and 'win' the encounter with Denise.

Use the following suggestions only *if you do not have your own ideas about how to keep the dialogue going.*

Denise, I am sorry you're annoyed, but you don't know as much as Bob about the work of the section.

I know more about this section than you do!

The problem was a technical one; you can't be expected to be able to help with that.

Bob is a good mate. Are you suggesting I shouldn't chat about work with him?

You're obviously so busy getting to grips with the job – I didn't want to bother you.

ROLE PLAY: DENISE, PHILIP, BOB

Brief – Bob

You haven't much time for women bosses in traditionally 'masculine' jobs. You are secretly quite pleased that Denise's staff are still coming to you for advice. It proves your point in a way. You are flattered that Philip still sees you as the *real* boss of his section. You and Philip meet socially and are both members of the company cricket team.

Your task is to maintain a dialogue with Denise which makes it difficult for her to reduce her anger at the situation. Patronize; imply that she can't do the job; try to joke her out of it, etc.

Please use your own ideas if possible. If undecided how to proceed, try some of the following suggestions.

'Come on Denise; aren't you over-reacting?'

'Look, love, as soon as you find your feet, Philip will toe the line – he's a good lad really.'

'Philip and I are mates. Are you suggesting that we can't discuss our jobs outside work?'

'I'm only trying to help – I know the job backwards. You should be grateful.'

'For goodness' sake, smile – it may never happen!'

ROLE PLAY: DENISE, PHILIP, BOB

Observer's brief

Please familiarize yourself with *The Scene.* Denise needs to name her anger, explain the reasons for it, and state firmly and forcibly what she wants to happen. Her tone, volume of voice, facial expression need to match her words. She may well need to practise broken record until her message has been received and understood. Both Philip and Bob have been asked to make life as difficult as possible for her. They should patronize her, make little of the matter, undermine her and generally be unwilling to accept what she has to say.

Observe the interactions carefully. See how well Denise copes. At the end of the role play, you will be asked to give Denise *positive and constructive* feedback on her performance.

Keep these questions in mind while watching the exchanges.

Did Denise state her anger, or just show it by her tone of voice and actions?

Did the intensity of Denise's response match the situation at all times?

Did she go in 'all guns blazing' when a milder initial approach might have been more appropriate?

What did Denise's body language tell you about how she was feeling?

What did she do well? What could she have done differently?

Any other comments?

ROLE PLAY: DENISE, PHILIP, BOB

Trainer's notes

Besides 'anger' there could be issues such as sexism here, which you may or may not want to follow up.

Firstly, ask the 'actors' how they felt the interaction went, beginning with Denise.

Did she actually *feel* the anger she was asked to present at any time? Why? What, in particular, made her especially cross?

Did she find it difficult or easy to name her anger? Why? Did she find any problems keeping on track – addressing the issue in hand? What went well? With hindsight, what would she have done differently? Did she feel she had 'won'?

Next, ask Philip and Bob for their comments. If this had been a real life matter, would they now act differently as the result of their meetings with Denise? Why? What did Denise handle well? If you had been Denise, is there anything you would have done differently?

Finally, using the questions on the Observer's brief as a prompt if it is helpful, get the reactions of those who watched the interactions, adding your own observations.

If possible, allow the 'actors' to perhaps change roles, and follow up this role play with more practice.

18

The confidante

THE SCENE

Carol confides in Ruth: 'Don't say anything to anyone, but I'm looking for another job. It's not that I'm unhappy here – far from it – but Clive is going to be made redundant next month, and we just won't be able to manage on the money I'm getting here. I must look for a full-time job with more responsibility.'

Carol is surprised when, next day, she is called into her boss's office. 'Look Carol,' he says, 'I know it's difficult to make ends meet these days, especially with people losing their jobs right, left and centre, and we don't want to lose you just for the sake of a few pounds extra each week. I've been considering the situation, and have decided to offer you a full-time position in our returns section. It's a new post, so the job will be what you make it. It's a challenge, and will of course give you a substantial increase in salary. What do you say?'

Carol is flabbergasted, flattered – and furious with Ruth for breaking a confidence – all at the same time. 'I'm grateful for your considering me; could I talk it over with my partner, Clive, and let you know tomorrow?' she says.

She returns to her office, still hopping mad, to confront Ruth.

ROLE PLAY: CAROL AND RUTH

Brief – Carol

Once over the shock of the encounter with your boss, you will probably be pleased that you now might not *have* to look for work elsewhere, and will be promoted within a company you are familiar and happy with.

However, your overriding emotion at the moment is anger at Ruth for (obviously) going straight to the boss to tell him that you were looking for another job. Whatever her intentions, you feel you must have it out with her.

ROLE PLAY: CAROL AND RUTH

Brief – Ruth

You realize that Carol had told you, in confidence, about her intentions to leave. However, you thought that you would be doing her a favour if the boss could find a way of allowing her to earn more within the company. You told the boss not to divulge that you had gone to him, and you are cross that he handled the situation with so little tact.

Your task is to apologize, explain, give excuses, be angry, be upset or whatever it takes to get Carol to back down and – if possible – apologize to *you* for *her* anger.

If possible, act out the role play without using the suggestions below. However, if you need ideas here are some you could use.

'I didn't say anything – he must have guessed.'

'You should be pleased. I did for you what you were too weak to do for yourself – ask for a rise.'

'You're so ungrateful. I did what I did in your best interest, and now you won't have to look for another job.'

'I really enjoy working with you, and couldn't bear the thought of you leaving. I did it because we're friends; please don't be cross.'

ROLE PLAY: CAROL AND RUTH

Observer's brief

Please read *The Scene*. Ruth has been briefed to offer all manner of excuses, to get angry or upset, to deny or explain and so on. The fact is that Carol needs to express her anger and let Ruth realize why she is so annoyed with her, while recognizing Ruth's needs too. If Ruth is 'demolished' in the process, Carol has not behaved assertively, but aggressively.

Observe the interaction. You will be asked to give your comments on the above, and your opinion of the exchange, after the role play. Keep the following points in mind.

Was Carol's tone, volume, facial expression and body language appropriate for what she said?

Did she give Ruth the opportunity to give her point of view?

Did she listen, and respond appropriately to what Ruth said?

Did Carol ever resort to sarcasm? Did her assertive stance ever topple into the aggressive mode? If so, what evidence do you have for this opinion?

What did Ruth's body language tell you about how she was feeling?

What did Carol do well? What wasn't so good? What could she have done differently?

Any other comments?

ROLE PLAY: CAROL AND RUTH

Trainer's notes

Process the role play by, first, asking Carol for her comments on how the role play went. Was it hard to stay angry with Ruth? Why? Did Ruth say anything which threw her? What went well? With hindsight, what would she have done differently?

Next, ask Ruth for her interpretation of the role play. Did she feel that Carol's tone of voice, etc. was appropriate? Did she get a chance to put her own position across? Did she feel that she'd been listened to? If this had been real life, what would her feelings now be for Carol? If she had been playing Carol, what would she have done differently?

Finally, using the Observer's brief as a prompt if this helps, ask the observers for their comments, ensuring that the feedback given is positive and constructive.

19

The absent-minded professor

THE SCENE

Angus is a medical photographer. He is employed by one of the leading teaching hospitals in Eastborough. He hasn't a boss, as such, but is there to provide a service for the hospital. His work involves photographing 'before', work-in-progress, and 'after' shots of surgical cases, making slides of X-rays for case reports, and keeping photographic records of some accident cases brought into casualty.

Sometimes he is asked to make slides for lectures. This has been the cause of some stress for him, because one professor in particular always leaves the subject of visual aids for his talks to the very last minute, putting additional workload pressure on Angus.

Yesterday this happened again. Angus had more than enough work to do for his consultants, some of which was urgent. Professor Wright came into Angus's studio first thing in the morning in his usual panic. He needed 36 slides made for the evening lecture. Angus tried to explain, assertively, that he had other urgent work, but Professor Wright 'pulled rank' and insisted that his work take priority over that of the consultants. Angus worked through his lunch-hour to complete the slides. He left them in a sealed envelope on Professor Wright's desk by 4.00 p.m., leaving the professor enough time to check and load the slides for the 6.00 p.m. lecture.

Angus met a student on his way in this morning, and asked how the lecture went – 'Were the slides any good?' he asked. 'Oh the lecture was cancelled,' the student said. 'Professor Wright told us yesterday morning that he had double-booked himself again, and had to go to a meeting with the administrator.'

Angus is furious, and decides to have it out with Professor Wright once and for all.

ROLE PLAY: ANGUS AND PROFESSOR WRIGHT

Brief – Angus

Although the professor is senior to the consultants, he is not your boss. However, you are employed to offer a service to the hospital, and to meet the needs of the doctors, surgeons, and all teaching staff. The tone of your approach should reflect this.

Your task is to express your anger in an appropriate way, and to try to prevent further occurrences of the kind which has caused you this inconvenience and unnecessary stress.

ROLE PLAY: ANGUS AND PROFESSOR WRIGHT

Brief – Professor Wright

Angus is understandably furious. He has put himself out, yet again, to accommodate you. You are always asking him to do last-minute jobs, when a little forward planning on your part could have avoided this. This time the rush was totally unnecessary. A telephone call from you, as soon as you realized that you were double-booked, could have halted the work. You are in the wrong and know it, and this in itself makes you more aggressive and prepared to defend yourself by attacking. Your brief is to be as awkward as possible for as long as possible!

If possible, use your *own ideas for the role play, but if you cannot think of any, here are some suggestions.*

'What's all the flap about? I'll use the slides when I reschedule the lecture next term.'

'I'm too busy to worry about every little thing; finalizing the report for my meeting with the administrator took priority over contacting every man and his dog about the lecture.'

'I put a notice on the board, saying the lecture was cancelled – what more do you expect?'

'The consultants' work isn't *that* urgent. It's not as if you were needed for an emergency yesterday, was it?'

ROLE PLAY: ANGUS AND PROFESSOR WRIGHT

Observers' brief

Please familiarize yourself with *The Scene*. The professor has been given the following brief:

You are always asking Angus to do last-minute jobs, when a little forward planning on your part could have avoided this. This time the rush was totally unnecessary. A telephone call from you, as soon as you realized that you were double-booked, could have halted the work. You are in the wrong and know it, and this in itself makes you more aggressive and prepared to defend yourself by attacking. Your brief is to be as awkward as possible for as long as possible!

Please keep this in mind while observing the interaction, and also consider the following points:

Did Angus express his anger in a manner appropriate to the situation? Is there anything you would have done differently?

Did Angus's body language and facial expression match his words and tone of voice?

What did Angus handle well? What could he have done differently or better?

Was the matter resolved in a mutually agreeable way?

Any other comments?

ROLE PLAY: ANGUS AND PROFESSOR WRIGHT

Trainer's notes

A difficult exercise because, although the professor is not Angus's boss he would obviously have status and clout with the authorities who employ Angus. Angus has every right to express his anger, and to try to avoid a recurrence of the event in question, but the vehemence with which he conducts the exchange has to reflect his position within the hospital.

The other element explored in this role play is the very real phenomenon of the person who knows they are in the wrong, appearing, not contrite, but equally angry. 'Attack is the best form of defence' in the maxim adopted by such people.

Process the role play by asking the 'actors' for their comments, beginning with Angus. Did he find it difficult to control himself? Why? Does he feel that he has made his point forcefully enough? What went well for him? Why? What, with hindsight, could he have handled differently?

Next, ask Professor Wright for his views of the role play. Given his brief, did he find it difficult to maintain his stance? Why? What did Angus handle well in the exchange? If he had been in Angus's shoes, what would he have done differently?

Finally, ask the observers for their comments. They could go through their prompt sheets if this is easier.

PART VIII

DEALING WITH SEXUAL HARASSMENT

PART VIII

DEALING WITH SEXUAL HARASSMENT

Despite improvements in management awareness, and the support of trade unions, sexual harassment is still a problem for a lot of women in the workplace – for some men too. Sexual harassment is difficult to define, because what some individuals see as harmless fun, others find embarrassing, offensive, or threatening. It is up to individuals to recognize their own innermost feelings, and to have the courage to communicate their objections if attention or comment directed at them is unwelcome.

In the first instance, it is important to express your views clearly and unambiguously to the perpetrator of the harassment, leaving them in no doubt that their remarks or attentions are offensive to you. If this approach fails, then the matter should be taken further, to management (or to a higher manager, if the 'offender' is your boss), to personnel, welfare, or to the unions.

Three things are important:

1. Make sure that the person who is harassing is in no doubt about the strength of your objection.
2. Make it clear what you intend to do if the harassment doesn't stop, i.e. you'll take it further.
3. Keep records with details of incidents, because cases of sexual harassment are often difficult to prove.

Finally, remember to use *all* your assertion skills, and ensure that tone of voice, body language and so on match your words.

EXAMPLE DIALOGUE

'Morning dear; how's my favourite girl today? Settling in well here, are you love?'

'Yes thank you Stan. My name's Mavis, by the way.'
'I know, I remember. "Stan", I said to myself, "that Mavis looks like your sort of girl." I think women look really sexy dressed in black – it really suits you.'

'Stan, I realize you think I should be flattered by that kind of remark, but actually, I find it embarrassing and offensive.'

'*Now* what have I done? I've never known a girl yet who hasn't responded to a bit of flattery, love. What's wrong with you?'

'Others may well be flattered – I find it offensive. Please don't make those kinds of remark to me, Stan – and my name's Mavis.'

20

It's a man's world

THE SCENE

When Jenny decided to study engineering, she realized that she would be working in a predominantly male domain. She considers herself broad-minded, and able to hold her own in a man's world.

Her new job is in a section where she is the only woman. Throughout college, and at her first place of employment, she has been able to ignore, laugh off, or deal with offensive comments, largely because she could communicate with the 'offender' on a one-to-one basis. Here, at Stower Bros., she is in difficulties, because the men, as a group, are harassing her. They made no secret of the fact that they:

a) Did not want to work with a woman.
b) Had no intention of altering their behaviour, language etc. because of her.
c) Consider it 'unnatural' for a woman to do their kind of work; also 'it takes jobs away from the blokes who need it'.

Consequently, they have made her life miserable for the two weeks she has been with them. They make sexist jokes at her expense. There has been a proliferation of 'girlie' pictures circulating, with accompanying lewd comparisons, which Jenny has tried to ignore. Her locker has been defaced with graffiti. Jenny has tried talking to the men as a group, and also individually, but has had no success. In fact, she feels now that the jokes, comments, and gibes are on the increase. Although angry that she hasn't been successful in handling this herself, she feels that she cannot penetrate their solidarity, so has to take the matter further. She makes an appointment to speak to the section head, Brian Manley, about it.

ROLE PLAY: JENNY AND BRIAN MANLEY

Brief – Jenny

You have a difficult task on your hands, because Brian, too, is only used to working with men, and is inexperienced in dealing with this sort of complaint. He is likely to try to dismiss your complaints as trivial, to make excuses for the men, or to make you feel that you are behaving in a 'typically female, hysterical way'.

Your task is to make him understand that sexual harassment is demeaning and potentially threatening to women; that you are serious in your complaint; and that what you are experiencing is not tolerable and must be stopped. Use all of your assertive skills to lead, and conclude a successful meeting where the outcome is satisfactory to you.

ROLE PLAY: JENNY AND BRIAN MANLEY

Brief – Brian Manley

You were not particularly happy with Jenny's appointment, although she was the best candidate for the job. You had foreseen difficulties within your team, but had kept apart, hoping that matters would resolve themselves in time. Personally, you sympathize with the men, and see no reason why they should moderate their language, curtail the telling of risqué jokes, or in any way change their way of working in order to accommodate Jenny. She wanted the job, and knew what she was letting herself in for.

Please use your own ideas to role play the meeting with Jenny. However, if you need help to start, here are some suggestions.

'OK, love, sit down and tell me all about it, then you'll feel better.'

'What do you expect *me* to do about it. It's your battle – you fight it!'

'If you can't stand the heat, you shouldn't be in the kitchen.'

'Look, your skills are excellent – you're as good as any man at the job – but shouldn't you think about looking for work that's more appropriate for a woman?'

ROLE PLAY: JENNY AND BRIAN MANLEY

Observer's brief

Please read *The Scene* through carefully. Jenny has a difficult task in that she must resolve the situation to her satisfaction. She will have to exercise all of her assertiveness skills, and also show some 'muscle' to convince Brian, whose sympathies are with the men, that he must, as the manager, discipline the men, making them aware of the possible consequences if they do not modify their behaviour.

Observe the interaction between Jenny and Brian, keeping in mind the following questions:

Was Jenny specific; did she come straight to the point in a businesslike way?

Did Jenny maintain good eye contact? Did she use a tone of voice, and volume, appropriate to the situation? What did her body language tell you about how she was feeling?

Did Jenny repeat herself, forcefully, until Brian accepted and understood what she was saying?

In your opinion, was the outcome successful from Jenny's point of view?

What did Jenny do that was particularly good? What, if anything could have been improved?

Any other comments?

ROLE PLAY: JENNY AND BRIAN MANLEY

Trainer's notes

If appropriate, some of the issues surrounding sexual harassment could be discussed here – such as why individuals find it hard to report sexual harassment, what to do if your complaints are ignored, and so on.

To process this role play, first ask the 'actors' how they found the role play. Was it difficult to act through? Why? If the harassment had involved a physical element, like a complaint about touching, or sexual propositions, would it have been more difficult? Why?

To Jenny: Was she happy with her performance? What went well? What was particularly difficult? Did she feel that she was in control throughout? Was she aware of her tone and volume of voice, body language and so on? Did she feel that at any time she might have been sending mixed messages? (e.g. the words were OK but force of delivery inappropriate)?

To Brian: What was good about Jenny's approach? If you had been in Jenny's shoes would you have done anything differently? If this had been real, do you feel the outcome might have been different? Why?

Finally, ask the observers to give their comments, using the Observer's brief questions if this helps.

21

Toy-boy

THE SCENE

James is a management trainee. His training involves working for set periods in each section of the organization. He has started in the post room, as his supervisor thinks that by collecting and delivering post, James will quickly obtain an insight into each department, and learn the names of his colleagues within the company.

James has a problem with one section – all women. Whenever he goes into this particular room, Gwen makes a bee-line for him! It's all done in fun, but she puts her arm around him and calls him her toy-boy, all to the amusement of the other women it seems. James finds it highly embarrassing, especially as now, when he goes to the staff canteen, some of the women and younger trainees point at him and laugh; word has obviously got round!

James has decided that enough is enough, and that he will have to speak to Gwen about the situation.

ROLE PLAY: JAMES AND GWEN

Brief – James

Gwen seems a pleasant enough sort of person, and you are sure she would stop her behaviour if she knew the real distress it was causing you. Your task is to make your position absolutely clear, while not putting her down in any way. At the end of the exchange, Gwen must be in no doubt about the seriousness of your complaint. The outcome must be satisfactory for you.

ROLE PLAY: JAMES AND GWEN

Brief – Gwen

James needs to resolve his problem with you. Your task is to make life as difficult as possible for him, for as long as is reasonable. Do this by any means you can think of: persist in flirting with him; refuse to take him seriously – try to joke him out of it; patronize him; get upset, or hurt, or angry, or outraged; deny his accusations, etc.

Try to use your own ideas to keep the role play going, but if you can't, here are a few suggestions to get you started.

'Oh come on James, pet – it's only a laugh!'

'Did anyone tell you that you look gorgeous when you're angry?'

'Grow up! Did you honestly think I fancied you? Don't flatter yourself!'

'I don't treat you any differently from anyone else. I've sons your age. If they can put up with a bit of teasing, so should you. No, I don't intend to change.'

'I'm upset that you should think I meant anything by it; I was just trying to be friendly, you being new here.'

ROLE PLAY: JAMES AND GWEN

Observer's brief

Please familiarize yourself with *The Scene*. After the role play, you will be asked to give your comments and advice to James. Keep the following questions in mind while observing the interaction.

In the role play, did James suggest the meeting should take place somewhere private?

Did James come straight to the point? Was this appropriate? Did he confuse the issue by giving a meandering preamble to his statements, or conversely, was he too abrupt?

Do you feel that James offered sufficient explanation? Did he treat Gwen with respect, while maintaining his own stance?

What observations have you on James's choice of words, tone of voice, eye contact, body language etc.?

What did James do well? How might his approach have been improved?

Do you feel that Gwen and James have resolved the matter in a mutually satisfactory way?

Any other comments?

ROLE PLAY: JAMES AND GWEN

Trainer's notes

Firstly, ask James for his comments on the role play. Did he find it easy or difficult to act out? Why? What, if anything, did Gwen do or say which he found difficult to cope with? Did he find himself slipping into either aggressive, or passive behaviour at any time? When was this? Why? What did he feel went well? With hindsight, what would he have done differently? Is he happy with the outcome?

Next, ask Gwen for her reaction to the role play. Did she feel that she had been treated with an appropriate degree of respect and sensitivity by James? Did she, at any point, think that she was 'winning' the exchange? If this had been a real event, does she think that Gwen would change her ways as a result of her talk with James? What did James do well? If she had been in James's shoes, what, if anything, might she have done differently?

Finally, ask the observers to go through their Observer's brief questions, giving their comments on the exchange between James and Gwen.

PART IX

DEALING WITH MONEY MATTERS

PART IX

DEALING WITH MONEY MATTERS

For many men, talking money seems to present few problems, but for some women, the subject is still taboo. They find it difficult to put a price on their services, or to ask, assertively, for fees which adequately represent their worth. Bartering or haggling would be anathema to most.

This is not to say that men always cope assertively with the topic of monetary self-worth and value. Interviewers will attest to the fact that the discussions of salary are often the most difficult part of a recruitment interview for the applicant. Fear of pricing yourself out of the running, or conversely, valuing yourself at too low a figure are inhibiting factors, as are appearing arrogant, or self-effacing.

People are naturally coy about mentioning money in the context of, 'What did you pay for ...?', or, 'How much is your ... worth?' and so on, and equally reticent about refusing to answer such questions.

Asking for money is difficult for most people, whether it is asking for an increase in salary, for a loan to be repaid, or even asking for your rights, as in the case of pensions or other living allowances.

Dealing with money matters calls for the best in assertiveness skills.

EXAMPLE DIALOGUE

'Annie, I'm in a bit of a fix. I've agreed to give a talk to the Cornelius Foundation next week – for a fee of course – but realize now that I just haven't the time to prepare for it. It needs some research into the organisation – especially its overseas operations. Would you be a pal and do the preparatory work for me?'

'Yes, I could give the project one or two days; how much are they going to pay you?'

'Not enough, considering their profit margins last year! That's great though, thanks a lot. When could we meet up to discuss it?'

'First, let's establish my fee. How much are they paying you to give the talk?'

'Not that much, considering the preparatory work that's needed – only £300.'

'Well, I'm prepared to do the research for £125 provided it takes no longer than one working day, plus the time for our meetings. I'll invoice you accordingly if that's OK.'

'Oh ... well ... alright then.'

Tg

22

The treasure

THE SCENE

Lisa has worked as secretary for a family business for the last five years. She took the job because it was near to her rural home, although the pay was poor compared with city salaries. The enterprize has grown steadily, although its profits are not tremendous and have been ploughed back into the business. Lisa is treated like one of the family – so much so that she too is expected to work unpaid overtime and forgo pay increases. Steve, the boss of the firm, tells everyone what a treasure she is, and constantly says that if he paid her what she was worth, the firm would be bankrupt. 'I don't know what I'd do without you – you run this place single-handed.'

This is all well and good, but Lisa has not had a rise for three years. In fact, her salary has fallen way behind even the local going rate for secretarial services.

Before she allows herself to become resentful, Lisa decides to speak to Steve about the situation, and to ask for a substantial increase in salary. She does her homework, and finds out that she should be expecting between £6 and £10 per hour. She is receiving just £4.50. While realizing Steve would have difficulty in meeting the top figure, she feels that £7 would be a reasonable sum to request.

ROLE PLAY: LISA AND STEVE

Brief – Lisa

Your task is to achieve agreement from Steve regarding a salary increase. Use your assertiveness skills to state your case, and arrive at an outcome which you would find satisfactory. This may well involve negotiation, so decide what compromises you would be prepared to accept, where you intend to stand firm, and what alternatives you might offer if Steve refuses your request.

ROLE PLAY: LISA AND STEVE

Brief – Steve

Although you know that Lisa's request is reasonable, and that she is worth it, and more, to your business, you feel you must try to talk her out of it – or at the very least, reduce the amount of the rise she proposes. Use every means you can think of to make it difficult for Lisa to persist in her claim.

Use your *own ideas if you can, but if you want help to start, here are a few suggestions.*

The logical approach: 'We just can't afford it. If I were to agree, our profit margin would be so reduced the viability of the business would be threatened.'

Play on her good nature: 'Lisa, I would love to pay you what you are really worth, but as it is, you receive more salary, in proportion, than I do myself. Now your rise just wouldn't be fair on my wife and kids would it?'

Try postponement: 'You've asked at a really difficult time. Can we talk about this again next month?'

Offer a compromise: 'I know you haven't had a rise in ages; how about an increase of 50p an hour immediately? That's £20 extra a week you know – then we'll look at the situation again next April in the new financial year.'

ROLE PLAY: LISA AND STEVE

Observer's brief

Please familiarize yourself with *The Scene*. After the role play you will be asked to give Lisa some constructive feedback about her performance. Keep the following questions in mind while you observe the interaction between Lisa and Steve.

Did Lisa manage to look Steve in the eye when she asked for a salary increase? Did she fidget, or show by her body language that she might be uncomfortable with the situation?

Did she make her request calmly and clearly? Was she specific? Did she give explanations? Did she apologize, at any time, for asking for a fair salary?

Was her tone of voice assertive? Did she show impatience, or become aggressive at any time? Alternatively, was she at any time too passive or accommodating of Steve's needs to the detriment of her own?

Did she show empathy? Did she listen to Steve's point of view, and acknowledge his position while maintaining her own? Did she stick to her point, or allow herself to be side-tracked?

What did Lisa handle well in the interaction? What might she have done differently, or better? If this had been a real office environment, do you think the outcome would have been mutually satisfactory, or did one side 'win'?

Any other comments?

ROLE PLAY: LISA AND STEVE

Trainer's notes

This role play includes many areas covered elsewhere – such as broken record, for example, asking for what we want, and negotiating.

To process the role play, first ask Lisa for her reactions. Did she find the task of asking for a rise easy or difficult? Why? In real life, would she find it more difficult to ask for a rise, in general terms, or to state *how much* money she wanted? Why?

In the role play, what, if anything, did Steve do or say which she found difficult to handle? Did she find it difficult to calmly repeat her request until it was accepted and understood? If a compromise was reached, was she happy with the result? What did she feel went well for her? How might her approach have been improved?

Next, ask Steve for his views. Did he feel that he was going to 'win' with Lisa? Did he, in fact, 'win' the encounter? Why (or why not)? What did Lisa do particularly well? If he had been in Lisa's shoes, what might he have done differently? If this had been real life, how might this encounter have affected the relationship between Lisa and Steve?

Finally, ask the observers for their comments, using the questions on the Observer's brief if this is helpful.

Note:
To give realism to the role plays, sums of money, rates per hour and so on have been included. The currency quoted is sterling, and approximate rates current at the time of publication are given. Please amend these details as necessary before using the role play with your group.

23

The price of friendship

THE SCENE

Following redundancy, Geoff has recently become self-employed as a builder/carpenter. Business hasn't been too bad, but he is not yet working to capacity. Hearing this, Jack, a golfing friend of his, asked Geoff if he would be prepared to take on a few repair jobs around his house.

One of the jobs on Jack's list is to find out what is causing the smell of damp in the conservatory, and to get the necessary repairs done. Geoff discovers that the base of one of the walls is rotten, and rainwater is seeping in from outside. He suggests to Jack that the wall be removed, the base bricked to a depth of three bricks before a new timber and glass wall is fitted. 'With care, I can use the existing glass and some of the frames – that will save you some money' Geoff said, 'the inside sills will have to be replaced. I've got some oak in my workshop which should be suitable.' Jack told Geoff to proceed with the work, adding: 'Let me know how much I owe you.'

Geoff completes the work, and Jack is so pleased with the result he says, 'I will recommend you to all my friends. However, he does not mention money. Geoff hadn't expected to invoice Jack and then wait ages for payment – he had expected Jack to settle up on the spot. He is short of working capital, so has to ask Jack for what he is owed.

ROLE PLAY: GEOFF AND JACK

Brief – Geoff

You are new to business, and realize now that you should have given Jack an estimate, explained what your hourly rate was, and so on, before you both agreed to proceed. You find it difficult asking for payment from anyone – it's far more difficult with friends. Jack may well ask for an invoice at some later stage, but you have this feeling that he has accepted the work as friend-to-friend. You will have lost not only working hours, but the cost of materials involved.

You itemize your costs which are as follows:

Labour	£120 (20 hours @ £6)
Materials	£100 (Receipts available)
Oak for sills	£15

Your task is to ask for, and get Jack to agree to, payment of £235 for labour and materials.

ROLE PLAY: GEOFF AND JACK

Brief – Jack

You were reluctant to agree to Geoff doing the work because he is so new to business, but as a friend you were prepared to give him some practice, especially as his order book was far from full. You had expected to pay for additional materials, but as Jack did not mention payment, you assumed that he was doing you a favour as a friend. You were very grateful, and fully intended to use your influence to recommend his work – which is excellent.

You are therefore surprised, hurt, offended, annoyed, etc. when Geoff asks for payment in full – at the going hourly rate – plus the cost of all materials.

Your task is to resist agreeing to payment – certainly in full – for as long as is reasonable.

Use the following suggestions only *if you are unable to keep the role play going.*

'I fully expected to pay for additional materials, but £100! I thought you said you could use existing glass, etc.'

'What's this item "oak sills"? I distinctly remembered you saying you had some oak in your workshop which you could use.'

'What do you charge your enemies? £6.00 an hour – to a friend? I could have employed a proper builder for less!'

ROLE PLAY: GEOFF AND JACK

Observer's brief

Please familiarize yourself with *The Scene*. After the role play, you will be asked to comment on the interaction between Geoff and Jack. Keep the following questions in mind:

Did Geoff apologize, over-apologize, fail to make eye contact, or give any other indication that he was not comfortable with the situation? If so, how could his approach have been improved?

Was he specific, or was he long-winded, faltering or did he waffle in any way? Did he give calm, clear explanations? Did he re-iterate his statements until heard, understood and accepted by Jack?

Did Geoff listen to Jack's point of view? Did he show empathy? Did he accept any criticism *which was justifiable*, in an assertive way?

What is your opinion of the outcome – was it satisfactory to both parties?

What did Geoff do well. If you had been Geoff, is there anything which you might have done differently?

Any other comments?

ROLE PLAY: GEOFF AND JACK

Trainer's notes

It may be appropriate to stress that we often put off dealing with things we find difficult, embarrassing, or threatening. Almost inevitably this procrastination only makes things worse for everyone concerned. In this case, if money and terms of working had been discussed openly from the outset, Geoff's difficulties would have been, at worst, lessened and, at best, resolved before friendship suffered.

To process the role play, first ask Geoff for his reaction to the exchange. Did he find it difficult, or relatively easy? Why? With the given circumstances, Geoff helped create his own problems. In the role play, did he feel that he had handled Geoff's own failings appropriately? Had this been real life, would he have been happy with the outcome? What went well? With hindsight, could he have done anything differently which might have improved matters?

Next, ask Jack for his views. With the given circumstances, did he feel that Jack was justified in feeling indignant, hurt, etc.? Did he feel that he had 'won' or 'lost' the exchange? Why? What did Geoff handle well? If he had been Geoff is there anything which he would have said or done differently? If this had been real life, does he think that the friendship of Jack and Geoff might have suffered, or been strengthened?

Finally, ask the observers for their comments.

Note:
To give realism to the role plays, sums of money, rates per hour and so on have been included. The currency quoted is sterling, and approximate rates current at the time of publication are given. Please amend these details if necessary before using the role play with your group.

24

What am I worth?

THE SCENE

Diane Fox is a training consultant. She worked in both the private and public sectors, in various management functions, for several years before going freelance. Most of her work has been with companies with whom she forged links while in full-time employment, so she knew their systems – and the fees they were prepared to pay for consultants' services.

Recently, however, these firms have relied more and more on in-house expertize, so Diane has decided that she must market herself with other, unfamiliar organizations. She has written to several local companies, asking for a meeting, and has received a reply from a Malcolm Henry at Mast Pharmaceuticals. He is interested in running some courses for his sales team, and has asked Diane to attend a meeting to discuss these.

The meeting goes well; Diane is sure she has convinced him that she has the ability to write and run the programmes. The point has come in the meeting to discuss finer details, like timings, resources – and fees! Diane wants to ask more than her usual £250 a day. She knows that other consultants charge far more than that, but does not know what Mast's will be prepared to pay.

ROLE PLAY: DIANE FOX AND MALCOLM HENRY

Brief – Diane Fox

You cannot begin work on the preparation of the courses for another four weeks, because of prior commitments. You should be ready to run the pilot programme six weeks after that.

The resources you will need are:

- duplicating facilities for handouts, etc.
- printing facilities for user manuals
- purchase/hire of training videos

In addition to the above are the usual incidentals needed to run a training course – paper, flipchart, folders, overhead projector and transparencies, and so on. All of this you expect the company to provide.

You hope that Mr Henry will tell you what he is prepared to pay for your services. You would like to receive £350 for every full day's training, plus £200 per working day for preparation time and meetings.

Your task is to conclude the meeting to your satisfaction. You *should not* agree to do the work for less than your previous fee of £250. Use your assertiveness skills to ask for what you want.

Good luck!

ROLE PLAY: DIANE FOX AND MALCOLM HENRY

Brief – Malcolm Henry

You are impressed with Diane Fox. Initially, you want to contract her to write and run one course, with the possibility of more commissions if her work is satisfactory.

You are prepared to finance the resources needed for the course, with the exception of the duplicating of course material which you feel should be inclusive in Diane's fee.

Regarding this fee, you expect Diane to name her figure. You are prepared to negotiate up to £400 per day, but expect to acquire her services for a lot less – especially as this is, in a way, a trial run.

Your task is to reach a mutually agreeable conclusion to the meeting. Please begin the role play at the point where details of the proposed training has been decided. You only need to negotiate three things:

1. Timings for the course – you would like the pilot to be run in two months' time.
2. Resources for the course (see above).
3. Fees (see above). You will need to be invoiced. Payment will be made on the last day of the month following the month the invoice was submitted.

In this role play it is Diane's assertiveness which is being tested. Don't be a pushover! It is up to you whether you choose to be assertive, or veer towards the aggressive in your approach.

ROLE PLAY: DIANE FOX AND MALCOLM HENRY

Observer's brief

Please familiarize yourself with *The Scene*. After the role play, you will be asked to give constructive feedback to Diane. Please keep the following questions in mind when observing the interaction.

Did Diane appear comfortable and relaxed talking about funding resources, and setting fees? What did she do or say to give this impression?

Was she specific in her requests? Did she use 'I' statements or did she tend to generalize? Did she try to justify her fee?

What feedback can you give Diane on her negotiating skills? What did she do particularly well? If you had been in Diane's shoes, would you have done or said anything differently?

Did Malcolm Henry call Diane, Miss (or Ms) Fox, or 'Diane'? Did Diane call him Malcolm, or Mr Henry? What would be the implications if she had used his title, while he called her by her first name?

Any other comments?

ROLE PLAY: DIANE FOX AND MALCOLM HENRY

Trainer's notes

The final question on the observer's brief poses the question of the appropriateness of using first names in formal business settings. This can be discussed further, but the point which needs to be made here is that concerning status and authority. Children are referred to by their first names, but they are expected to address adults as Mr, Mrs or Miss. But an unequal interaction is caused if one person, say, Mrs Smith, retains her title when addressing another person, say, Julie Brown, merely as 'Julie'. In this role play, it would be important for both parties to generate an equal relationship by using first names, or surnames. If it is played as 'Diane' and 'Mr Henry', Diane's status, and therefore confidence, is subtly undermined.

To process the role play, first ask the 'actors' for their views of the interaction. Did Diane find talking about money easy or difficult? Why? Did Malcolm feel at ease asking about fees? Why? What went well for Diane in the negotiation? What might have been handled differently, or better? Was the outcome mutually satisfactory?

Finally, ask the observers for their comments. Go through the Observer's brief questions if this helps. Ensure that constructive, positive feedback is given, with the opportunity for the protagonists to follow up this role play if possible.

Note:
To give realism to the role plays, sums of money, rates per hour and so on have been included. The currency quoted is sterling, and approximate rates current at the time of publication are given. Please amend these details if necessary before using the role play with your group.

PART X

SELF-ASSERTION

PART X

SELF-ASSERTION

The final role play in this manual is slightly different from the others. It can involve all members of the group, certainly in the planning stage if not in the actual practice of the self-assertion – this would depend on the time available and the number in the group.

Because of previous experiences and childhood conditioning, most of us find it difficult to sing our own praises. We are afraid of offending people, of appearing conceited, boastful, egotistical or superior. However, there are occasions when we should set modesty aside and assert our qualities, achievements, skills and attributes in a positive and forceful way. The recruitment interview is one such occasion. To succeed, a candidate should appear to the interviewer as someone self-assured and confident; someone who 'can', not someone who 'thinks they might be able to'. This confidence has to be choreographed however, so that words, actions and all non-verbal communication combine to present someone able and assured, yet not too casual, arrogant, pompous or pushy – in other words, an assertive approach is called for.

In order to present ourselves in such a way, we need to do some homework on our qualities and strengths. Like any good salesperson, we must know the product from A to Z, and become skilled in selling its good points. In this case, of course, the product we are selling is ourselves.

25

Sales talk

TRAINER'S NOTES

The role plays concern being interviewed, and will ask individuals to sell their strengths to others. The setting is immaterial – a recruitment interview, a promotion interview, internal or external. The point of the exercise is to enable individuals to recognize their value, *and name, in an assertive way*, their attributes and skills.

Firstly, allow group members some time to list what they are good at. These will be skills and attributes, work or socially based. For individuals normally reluctant to think about themselves in a positive way, this can be a daunting and difficult task, so the time needed for this, and the support given by the trainer will obviously differ from group to group.

Options

Either divide groups into triads, so that each individual has the chance to interview, be interviewed and to give feedback; *or* ask for volunteers to be interviewed in front of the whole group; or explain that everyone will be interviewed in front of the whole group. A group member or the trainer could conduct these interviews. The option you choose will depend on the cohesion and supportiveness of the group, the confidence of individuals, the time available, and so on.

ROLE PLAY: THE INTERVIEW

Interviewee's brief

In the space below, write down as many things as you can that you are good at. For example: 'I am well organized', 'I am a good listener', 'I am loyal', 'I relate well to children' etc.

I AM GOOD AT:

Next, think of your skills. What can you do? List these. For example: 'I can operate a word processor; 'I can do my own car maintenance'; 'I am numerate'; 'I can cook' etc.

THESE ARE MY SKILLS:

ROLE PLAY: THE INTERVIEW

Interviewer's brief

The type of interview you are conducting is immaterial. It doesn't matter what sort of job is being applied for. You are to ask any of the following questions to test the individuals' ability to 'sell' themselves assertively:

1. 'Why do you think you are right for this job?'
2. 'What do you consider to be your strengths?'
3. 'There are several applicants for this position; why should we employ you?'
4. 'Why should I include you on my shortlist?'

ALL of these questions require interviewees to sell their strengths – to articulate their value, their skills and positive qualities – to show self-assertion.

To keep the role play going, ask probing questions too, using who-what-why-when-how type open questions. Also:

- 'What else?' (to encourage interviewee to give further examples).
- 'Go on' (as above).
- 'Can you give me an example?' (to give the interviewee the opportunity to back up their assertion).

ROLE PLAY: THE INTERVIEW

Observer's brief

Please consider the following points in order to give the interviewee constructive feedback after the role play.

What was the physical setting of the mock interview – were the chairs of similar height? Was the distance between them appropriate? What about the angle of the chairs? Could the interviewee have done anything to make the situation either more equal, or more comfortable?

Did the interviewee sit in an assertive way, i.e. upright, relaxed, open posture? If not, did they tend to be too casual or tense? How did this show itself? Was eye contact appropriate? Did they tend to look at the floor, or their hands rather than at the interviewer when responding to questions? Was the gaze perhaps too constant? What impression might this give an interviewer? How did they use their hands throughout the interview? Were they used appropriately to demonstrate enthusiasm, but without excessive gestures? Were they gripped nervously, or clasped in a relaxed way?

Did they assert their attributes and skills in a confident way? Was the tone of voice appropriate? Did they use 'I think' statements or 'I can' assertions? Did they use any 'My boss (or partner, or mother, etc.) says that I'm good at ...' type statements?

Any other comments?

ROLE PLAY: THE INTERVIEW

Trainer's notes

How you process the role plays will depend on how you chose to conduct them. If triads were used, the processing has to take place with the trainer circulating around these sub-groups, offering guidance, support and feedback on an individual basis. General comments and observations can be made in plenary after everyone has had the chance to be interviewed.

If, however, either of the other options is chosen, it may be easier to use the questions put in the Observer's brief as a guide to the processing, pulling out different aspects as appropriate.

Whichever method is chosen, the interviewee must be given positive and constructive feedback, with, if possible, the opportunity to follow up this role play with more practice in self-assertion.